$29.95

CELEBRITY ★ CHEFS

BOBBY FLAY

Bobby Flay

Don Rauf

Enslow Publishing

101 W. 23rd Street
Suite 240
New York, NY 10011
USA

enslow.com

Published in 2016 by Enslow Publishing, LLC
101 W. 23rd Street, Suite 240, New York, NY 10011

Library of Congress Cataloging-in-Publication Data
Rauf, Don.
  Bobby Flay / Don Rauf.
    pages cm. — (Celebrity chefs)
  Summary: "Describes the life and career of chef Bobby Flay"— Provided by publisher.
  Includes bibliographical references and index.
  ISBN 978-0-7660-7172-8
  1. Flay, Bobby—Juvenile literature. 2. Cooks—New York (State)—New York—
Biography—Juvenile literature. 3. Restaurateurs—New York (State)—New York—
Biography—Juvenile literature. 4. Celebrity chefs—United States—Biography—
Juvenile literature. I. Title.
  TX649.F54R28 2016
  641.5092—dc23
  [B]
                            2015026890
Printed in the United States of America

Photo Credits: Cover, p.1 Ethan Miller/Getty Images for Vegas Uncork'd by Bon Appetit/
Getty Images; pp.4, 7, 88 Helga Esteb/Shutterstock.com; p.9 Jon Bilous/Shutterstock.
com; pp.11, 14, 22, 23, 24, 37, 44, 53, 60, 68, 94 © AP Images; p. 17 Bernstein Associates/
Getty Images; p. 19 Maria Bastone/AFP/Getty Images; p.26 Stephen Lovekin/
WireImage/Getty Images; p.28 Evan Sung; p. 30 Arthur Schatz/Life Magazine/The LIFE
Picture Collection/Getty Images; p.32 A.J. Wilhelm/National Geographic Creative; p.34
Roman Cho/Getty Images; p.41 Alex J. Berliner/ABImages via AP Images; pp.42, 56
Food Network/Courtesy: Everett Collection; p.49 Amy Mayer; p.62 Robin Marchant/
Getty Images; p.64 Charles Eshelman/FilmMagic/Getty Images; p.71 Manny Carabel/
Getty Images; p.74 Gregory Pace/FilmMagic/Getty Images; p.77 © Vespasian/Alamy;
p.81 PRNewswire; p.83 Joe Kohen/FilmMagic/Getty Images; p.86 Larry Marano/Getty
Images; p. 98 Paduk/Shutterstock.com; p. 99 Delerium Trigger/Shutterstock.com; p.
101 ©iStockphoto.com/mofles; p. 104 Zoryanchik/iStock/Thinkstock; p.106 milarka/
iStock/Thinkstock; p. 108 Joshua Resnick/Shutterstock.com; p.110 Bill Hogan/Chicago
Tribune/TNS via Getty Images; p. 112 ©iStockphoto.com/boblin; p 114 magnolia/
Shutterstock.com; p. 115 Ahturner/Shutterstock.com.

CONTENTS

★

Bobby Flay has parlayed his success as a chef into a national TV and restaurant empire.

Chapter

1

A Chef
Takes Shape

Bobby Flay seems to live his life at full boil. He is a chef who is constantly in motion, and somehow he seems to be everywhere at the same time. Turn on the Food Network and you're likely to see Flay hosting or competing in a number of shows. At the same time, he is in charge of a small and growing restaurant empire with eateries in New York City, Las Vegas, Atlantic City, and the Bahamas. Not only does he oversee the restaurants, Flay is often in kitchen—chopping, frying, baking, and preparing the dishes for those who love his unique style of cooking. Plus, he operates almost twenty hamburger places around the country. His cookbooks can fill a shelf in a library, and his name graces a major line of cooking-related gear. Most people would be exhausted following Flay's busy schedule, but Flay usually appears calm and in control at the center of the storm. What drives Flay? It's always his passion for cooking. Flay loves making food so much that he does it both to work and to relax.

5

Born Into the Business

With red hair and freckles, Robert William Flay came barreling into the world on December 10, 1964, in New York City. Flay is a New Yorker through and through. He has a long family history in the Big Apple. At least five generations of his family have lived in the area. Flay is the only child of Dorothy Flay, a paralegal who lives in New Jersey, and Bill Flay, who was an attorney but changed careers to become a restaurant manager. The couple split up when Flay was just five years old, but Flay has great memories of grilling with his parents on the New Jersey shore. These fond memories of beach grilling may have set him on course to become a grill master later in his life.

His father may have given him the cooking gene. His dad worked in the restaurant business in Manhattan. Bill managed two successful eateries—a rustic Italian place called Orso, and Joe Allen's, which serves up American cuisine in New York City's theater district. Both restaurants continue to operate to this day. Joe Allen's might be the more famous of the two. It has been a hangout for Broadway stars and theatergoers for decades. The restaurant serves classic American food from steaks to seafood, and when it came to eating, Bobby got his fare share of well-prepared steaks and burgers.

Despite the divorce, Bobby was raised in comfort. He grew up not having to worry about money on the Upper East Side of Manhattan. But Flay was not exactly a sheltered rich kid. He liked to mix things up on the streets of New York. The young Yankee fan had a lot of street smarts. He liked to play basketball, and he tended to hang out with the tougher kids in the neighborhood. He played the card game blackjack on front stoops. He occasionally got into fights with kids in other

Bobby Flay's parents divorced when he was young, but he had the support of both his mom and his dad.

neighborhoods. Sometimes the fights would get a little rough, with some kids bringing knives or chains.

Although he wasn't set on a career in food when he was young, he was interested in cooking. He organized his mother's grocery lists and concocted snacks to munch on after school. He made deviled eggs with his mom and My*T*Fine chocolate pudding. In an interview with Dorothy Cann Hamilton, founder of the International Cooking Center, Flay said that his mother's idea of gourmet cooking was frying a pork chop and opening a jar of Mott's applesauce. She would "gourmet it up" by adding cinnamon.[1]

When he was eight, he asked for an Easy-Bake Oven for Christmas. His father thought a G.I. Joe would be more appropriate for a boy, so Bobby wound up getting both. As a boy, Bobby worked for a short time as a child model, but it really didn't interest him. Modeling required a lot of sitting still, and Bobby wasn't one for sitting still. With a growing love of food, the sixth-grade Flay went to work in a pizza parlor—Mimi's on the Upper East Side near his home. (Mimi's is still open today.) He delivered pies and grated cheese. Flay is still proud that he delivered the pies on time. He liked Mimi's pizza so much that he used to hang out there and eat pizza after school. He also scooped ice cream at Baskin-Robbins for a brief time.

While Flay may have been an early star in his family's kitchen and at work, he was not a star in school. He went to the Catholic school, St. Francis Xavier High School, not far from where he would open his first restaurant. He tried to play on the school basketball team, but reportedly did not like taking orders from the coach, so he stopped. He started cutting classes to go to the racetrack. He soon dropped out altogether at age seventeen. Flay jokes that he did go to college though:

Flay grew up on Manhattan's Upper East Side. Flay encountered all different kinds of people in New York, and this interest in other people and their cultures has served him well as a chef.

His college was UCLA, or the University on the Corner of Lexington Avenue. He also filled a lot of his hours playing pool. He had his own pool cue, and his passion for the game continues to this day. In fact, he keeps a poolroom in his house. It fuels his nonstop competitive nature, but he also enjoys playing by himself. He says he can relax and plan the next day while playing pool alone.

Getting Busy

When he dropped out of school, Flay said he went to work immediately because he didn't want to waste his time. One day when he was 18, his father called Bobby in to work because a busboy at Joe Allen's needed two weeks off to visit his sick grandmother.

As Bobby recalled later, his father basically ordered him into work, but it was a fateful moment. When the busboy returned, the chef decided to keep Bobby on. Bobby agreed to work, but at the time, he just did if for the money and to please his father. He didn't do it because of any strong desire to work in a restaurant.

He hustled as a busboy and then a dishwasher, but he wasn't very reliable at first. He would often arrive at work late and leave early. He thought that because he was the manager's son, he could have that flexibility. That's when his father sat him down to have a little talk. Bill said that if he was going to drop out of school and work, he'd have to show up on time and work hard. Although Bobby liked the restaurant atmosphere well enough, he didn't think a life as a chef was necessarily the path he should follow.

In an interview in the New York Post, Flay said, "I just thought it was cool that somebody was paying me to do something. I wasn't exactly enthralled by it. But three or four months later I remember just waking up and being excited about going to work." The light bulb came on for Bobby. He had a realization that he liked the kitchen. He liked learning in that setting. He liked that he was accomplishing something.[2]

> *"I remember just waking up and being excited about going to work."*

Flay was motivated much more by this type of work than he had been by school. Because of this experience, he believes in vocational schooling. In fact, later on in his life, Flay taught a culinary class at a high school in Long Island City, Queens, and realized "not everyone learns the same way." Flay wishes there would be more of this type of hands-on education offered in schools. He says that there's a need for cooks in the world and cooking classes in high schools would help. After working a short time at Joe Allen's, Flay moved up to a position as a kitchen helper. He was in charge of the salad station, where he cleaned the lettuce and made the salad dressing. He would make gallons of a curried dressing for a curried chicken salad every day. Because Joe Allen himself was hugely successful as a restaurant owner, Flay was getting an inside view of what it is like to run a thriving independent eatery. Joe Allen operated three Joe Allen's restaurants (in New York City, Paris, and London) and four Orso restaurants (in New York City, Los Angeles, Toronto, and London).

Bill Flay was a successful Manhattan restaurant manager. He ran the famous theater district eatery Joe Allen, which is still in operation today. Bill pulled some strings to get Bobby his first food-related job in the restaurant.

Five Kitchen Tools That
★ Bobby Flay Loves

In an interview in StarChefs.com, Flay said that these were the five tools he must have in the kitchen:

1. Squeeze bottles for sauces and vinaigrettes.
2. A high quality but simple pair of tongs. (Grilling tongs are always awkward so go for the basic kind.)
3. Three knives—a chef's knife, a paring knife, and a boning knife. He uses Global knives. They are stainless steel and are made in Japan.
4. A small metal spatula.
5. A good side towel. [3]

Learning His Chops

Just as Flay was noticing all the aspects of restaurant life, Joe Allen was noticing Flay. Allen now saw a young man who had gotten his act together and was very industrious and dedicated to his job. Because he saw such potential in Flay, Allen offered to pay Flay's way to attend the new French Culinary Institute, which was just opening in the SoHo neighborhood of Manhattan. Allen was willing to invest the $6,800 in Flay's tuition because he said that maybe one day Flay would be an asset to him down the line. "Joe was very good at paying it forward," Flay said in an interview with Dorothy Hamilton on the podcast *Chef's Story*. "I've learned from his good will to use some of that in what I do now. I think it's really important to pay it forward." And Joe Allen gave him some advice that Flay remembers to this day. He told him that he might not get this now, but cooking can take you anywhere in the world.

Flay's initial reaction to Allen's offer, however, was negative. He didn't want to go back to school; he wanted to keep working. But he had caught the cooking bug, and ultimately he decided that if he were going to get ahead as a chef he should go ahead with the plan. Flay was missing one thing before he could attend the culinary institute: a high school diploma. So he put in the extra time outside of work and earned his high school equivalency diploma.

When Flay started the six-month program at the school in 1983, the culinary institute was literally still being built. The school was so new that there were just eleven students in his class when he started. And although Flay signed up for the program, he wasn't always a good student there either. In fact, he was voted "least likely to succeed" because he'd often cut classes at that school too. But Flay has said the French Culinary Institute was exactly what he needed. The institute helped to get his creative juices flowing. He couldn't learn through just textbooks—he needed to learn by doing, and that's exactly how they taught at the institute. Here, he mastered French cooking techniques. He discovered ways to cut, such as julienne, tournée, and chiffonade. He learned the French approach to preparing food, such as sautéing and

> *"I think it's really important to pay it forward."*

Flay was in the first graduating class of the French Culinary Institute (now the International Culinary Center) in New York City. His employer, Joe Allen, saw Flay's potential and offered to pay his tuition.

flambéing. Flay was in the very first graduating class of the Institute, in 1984 . (The school continues but it has since been renamed the International Culinary Center and has expanded to locations in California and Italy.) "Every day I cook in my restaurants, I'm using techniques that I learned at ICC," Flay said on the ICC website. "Every day. And I always will for the rest of my life."

Chapter
2

Putting on
the Apron

Whan he graduated in 1984, Flay started working as a sous chef at the now closed Brighton Grill on Third Avenue on the Upper East Side in Manhattan. The sous chef is the second in command in the kitchen, so when the executive chef at the Brighton Grill was suddenly fired, management turned to Flay. He had only been there a week but he quickly found himself in charge as an executive chef. Flay was going from the proverbial frying pan into the fire. He soon realized that he was in over his head. He held it together for about a year, but after twelve months in a high-pressure leadership position, the young chef was cracking. He just couldn't do it any more. He was exhausted emotionally, mentally, and physically. He was just twenty years old and he wasn't ready to keep up with such responsibility, so he left.

He wanted to get a position that was more entry level—a job where he could learn from others and develop the techniques he learned in school. "When you go to culinary school and you graduate successfully, you are not a chef," Flay said on *Chef's Story,* speaking about his personal experience at the Brighton

Grill. "Everybody thinks, that now you're a chef and you can cook anything you want. You actually have to go in the field and utilize the things that you've learned. And then the light bulb goes off and you say, 'Oh yeah, I did learn this technique at the French Culinary Institute or International Culinary Center."[1]

Flay recommends that every budding chef go to culinary school like he did because that's where a person learns the basics to eventually be able to create his or her own things. Then he recommends that new cooks coming out of culinary school take an entry-level position and avoid his mistake.

> *"When you go to culinary school and you graduate successfully, you are not a chef ... You actually have to go in the field and utilize the things that you've learned."*

Lessons from the Pros

In searching for a new opportunity, Flay went to a party at his old school, the French Culinary Institute. Here, he met chef Gail Anderson, who worked with the successful New York restaurateur Jonathan Waxman. Waxman was—and still is—a celebrated chef who originally came from Berkeley, California. He developed a style of cooking called Californian cuisine. This approach combines different styles of food (called fusion) plus local fresh ingredients. Flay told chef Anderson that he would love to work with Waxman, and on the spot, she agreed to give him a try. In an interview in The *Wall Street Journal*, Flay said that his enthusiasm convinced her.[2] He said he would give 120 percent—just tell him what to do, and

Chef Jonathan Waxman, one of the first proponents of California Cuisine, gave Bobby Flay one of his early starts. Waxman's love of Southwestern cuisine would have a great impact on Flay.

Flay would jump to it. He made it clear that he wanted to be trained and molded and today that's exactly what Flay looks for when he hires people.

Flay packed his knives and went to work with Waxman, who was the restaurateur and owner of Jams on the Upper East Side, Bud's on the Upper West Side, and also a French bistro called Hulot's. (Today, Waxman runs Barbuto in the West Village and a new version of his original Jams in midtown Manhattan.) Flay worked and learned at all three of these restaurants.

These were top, innovative eateries, so Flay was absorbing as much information as possible from the great young chefs who worked there. Being around those who are better than you is a great way to learn and improve your art. In the Food Network series *Chefography,* Flay said that Waxman was the first person to teach him what good food was. He thought Waxman appreciated his confidence and work ethic.

Specifically, it was the Mexican and Southwestern touch that chef Waxman brought to the menu at Bud's that fascinated Flay. At Bud's, the kitchen served up fried strips of blue corn tortillas, ripe avocado, beans, red and yellow peppers, salsas, hot chiles, and grilled scallions. These Southwestern flavors and Cajun styles made a huge impact on Flay that would shape his culinary career. Although Flay had never visited the Southwest and didn't even live in the Southwest of Manhattan, he liked the bright, colorful food with a sweet heat and bold flavors.

"It took a while for me to understand how much I really loved it," Bobby Flay said in an interview in *Ocean Drive.* "When I started working with the ingredients, I fell in love with them and decided to hone my skills [around these flavors and ingredients]." [3]

Flay also loved working as a line cook. He did it for years and loved the camaraderie. He loved the energy of it. He loved being in the heat of being busy. He felt like he was part of a team. He was always an athlete growing up and into his early adulthood, and cooking on a line gave him a similar feeling. "I loved being able to high-five someone next to me because we accomplished something," Flay said in *Catholic Online.* [4] "Now I'm the head coach. It's a little bit lonelier being the head coach."

Fed up with the long hours and low pay of the restaurant industry, Flay got a job on Wall Street. While working as a clerk at the American Stock Exchange, Flay realized how much he loved cooking. Being in the wrong job affirmed his desire to be a chef.

A Sudden Career Shift

In the mid 1980s, just as he was getting his cooking chops well-honed, he decided to make a shift. Yes, Flay was doing what he loved, but he saw all his friends getting rich on Wall Street. Wall Street at the time was booming, and many large fortunes were being made. At age twenty-one, Flay was making about $200 a week cooking. He often met his friends to play poker. "They were making a ton of money, and I was making eight

Bobby Flay's Advice on
⭐ How to Cook a Steak

In *Food & Wine* magazine, Flay gave this advice on grilling steak: "You need high heat and you need to let the grill do its job. Leave the steak alone. Let it get nice and crusty. Flip it once, and don't overcook it. Everybody says, 'I have problems overcooking steak on the grill,' but just take it off earlier!"

He has also said it is very important that when you put something on the grill, you leave it in place to cook. If you move it around too quickly, chances are it is going to stick. "I also recommend that you coat the food with canola oil. Canola oil is great and light when grilling." [7]

cents," Flay said in an interview in *Inc.* "They owned their one-bedroom apartments. That, for me, was like Shangri-la." [5]

He decided to hang up his chef's hat (at least for a while) and took a position as a clerk at the American Stock Exchange. He sat in bleachers that overlooked the stock exchange floor. He would answer the phones and the give hand signals to the broker on the floor to make various transactions. "I tried it for six months, but it so wasn't for me," Flay said in an interview in The *New York Post*. "No creativity to it at all." [6] He knew his best route to success was to follow his true passion. That was the only way he would be happy.

A Small "Miracle"

In 1988, Flay returned to the kitchen. He landed a job as executive chef at the Miracle Grill in Manhattan's East Village. Unlike his time at Brighton Grill, he was now seasoned and ready to take on the responsibilities of the top position. The restaurant also served the food that most interested him— Southwestern cuisine. Now, Flay had a chance to introduce the city his own take on this type of food. At this venue, which advertised itself as a cantina, Flay happily grilled up pork chops with an orange-ancho chile recado (a spicy paste linked to Mexican and Belizean cuisine). He also slung together catfish tacos, quesadillas, and savory grilled tuna.

When the Miracle Grill first opened, no one really seemed to care about it. The food was great but people were slow to hear about it. That all changed when *New York* magazine gave Miracle Grill a great review. Then the word spread like wildfire. Crowds were showing up in droves, and the cantina's garden proved to be a very popular draw in warm weather.

"Now I'm the head coach. It's a little bit lonelier being the head coach."

Flay was busy running the show at the Miracle Grill, but he was always curious and interested what other chefs were cooking up. So after exhausting nights at work, Flay would explore and take time to eat in other restaurants. He and his co-workers would try different eateries ranging from Chinese food to new Spanish cuisine. He remembers being impressed by the food at Les Halles, a French restaurant on Park Avenue South, run by the then up-and-coming chef Anthony Bourdain.

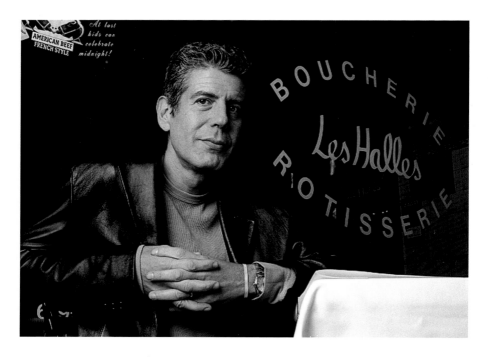

Anthony Bourdain was a young, exciting chef when Bobby Flay first ate at his restaurant Les Halles. Since that time, Bourdain has gone on to fame with his memoir *Kitchen Confidential* and his popular culinary adventure shows on the Travel Channel.

Flay also got his first taste of what it's like to be on TV while working at the Miracle Grill. His mother met TV talk show host Regis Philbin at a party. She told Regis about the great success her son was having. Not long after that party, the producers of *Live with Regis and Kathie Lee* gave Flay a call. He showed the dynamic morning duo and millions of TV viewers how to make the perfect potato salad. The experience gave Flay a peek into the power of being in front of the television camera.

Thanks to his mother, Flay was able to score an appearance on the popular morning show *Live with Regis and Kathie Lee*, which was broadcast to a national audience.

While working at Miracle Grill, Flay also met Debra Ponzek. Like Flay, Ponzek was a very hot chef. She was gaining rave reviews at Montrachet, a highly praised French restaurant in TriBeCa. He not only found Ponzek to be an amazing chef, he thought she was very attractive. A few weeks after meeting at a Meals on Wheels charity event, they started dating and eventually decided to get married. In the *New York Times*, Ponzek described Flay as a man who was decisive. He knew what he wanted and he went after it. Flay had eaten several times at Montrachet and loved Ponzek's food. It may have been love at first bite.

Flay met fellow chef Debra Ponzek of the Tribeca hotspot Montrachet. The two fell in love almost immediately due in part to their similar lifestyles.

Chapter
3

The Beginning of
an Empire

One night at the Miracle Grill, Jerry Kretchmer, a New York state assemblyman and owner of the Gotham Bar and Grill, came in to eat with his wife. Kretchmer had just returned from the Southwest, whose food and flavors had captivated him. After eating Flay's take on the cuisine, Kretchmer was very impressed. In fact, he was so swept away that he wanted to work with the young chef. Kretchmer arranged a meeting with Flay, where he suggested the two open a restaurant together. He told Flay that he would put up the money and get him press attention, and Flay just had to worry about the menu and keeping diners happy. They shook hands and a fruitful, long-lasting partnership was born. In 1990, Flay said goodbye to the Miracle Grill.

Flay and Kretchmer looked for spaces together and found a spacious venue along Fifth Avenue near 15th Street. They would call the restaurant Mesa Grill. Just before debuting his new restaurant to the world, Flay told the media, "I'm going to put a new and colorful twist on Southwestern cuisine."[1] He was ready

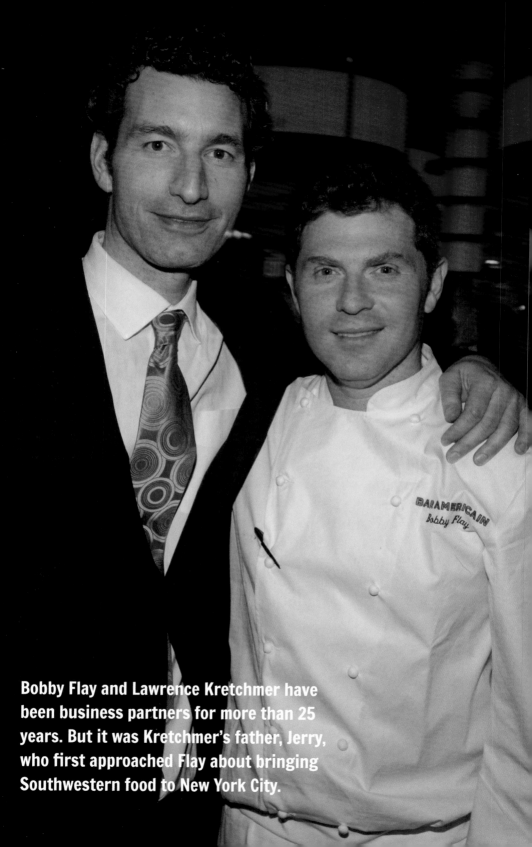

Bobby Flay and Lawrence Kretchmer have been business partners for more than 25 years. But it was Kretchmer's father, Jerry, who first approached Flay about bringing Southwestern food to New York City.

to give the New York palate a jolt with his spicy Southwestern flavors, and he'd be highlighting some ingredients that many Easterners were unfamiliar with. Dishes would feature a variety of rich and hot chiles. Many would come with jicama, a type of Mexican turnip that is crisp like an apple. At the time, few New Yorkers had ever heard of this exotic vegetable. They decorated the tall-ceilinged space in the theme of the West with cowboys and bucking broncos.

The Southwest Sets New York on Fire

Opening day was on January 15, 1991. Flay was just twenty-six years old. Unfortunately, that very day, the country was going to war with Iraq. Flay said that many people were not staying in the restaurant but taking their food home to watch news about the war on TV. He was basically looking out into an empty dining room on what should have been a triumphant night. Flay was dismayed, but he was not a quitter. He knew he had to stick with it—keep his head down and keep going. Over the next few months, the crowds started to come in.

Despite the turbulent times, things settled down and those hungry for something new and flavorful flocked to Mesa Grill. Southwestern flavors, at this time, were still something new. The food critic Gael Greene at *New York* magazine awarded Mesa Grill Best New Restaurant in 1992. The *New York Times* raved about the restaurant when it first opened and said "the sassy fare at Mesa Grill surpasses anything of its kind elsewhere in New York."[2] The praise continued, eight years later in 2000, the *Times* again gave the Mesa Grill high marks, awarding it two stars.

The menu was all about big, bold flavors. Sweet potato soup was accented with smoked chiles, maple crema, and macron

Mesa Grill, Flay's first restaurant, opened in 1991. He began as executive chef but soon became partner. Mesa Grill was an immediate hit, and New Yorkers were dazzled by his take on Southwestern food.

almonds. Sixteen-spice chicken came with cascabel chile sauce and tangerine relish. A chorizo-goat cheese tamale was served with sage butter. Other highlights were roasted corn with chipotle aioli, lime and cotija cheese and chile rellenos with orange sweet pepper sauces. For dessert, sweet and rich coconut bread pudding with coconut dulce de leche completed many meals. From fiery and cool to sweet and tart, Flay deftly combined zesty wet and dry rubs, bold sauces, along with creative and timeless techniques. Choices were plentiful and Flay was continuously adding and subtracting dishes. Other customer favorites were the spice-rubbed New York strip steak with house-made steak sauce, BBQ duck-filled blue corn pancakes with habañero sauce, grilled shrimp brushed with smoked chile butter and tomatillo salsa, and coffee-rubbed filets mignon with ancho-mushroom sauce.

To impress his bride-to-be, Debra Ponzek, Flay invited her and five of her friends to Mesa Grill. He dazzled the group with a deluxe dinner featuring cilantro soup, black-bean cakes, and shrimp with roasted garlic tamales.

Flay's Southwestern spin was a culinary sensation. In May 1993, Flay was voted the James Beard Foundation's Rising Star Chef of the Year, a prize that recognizes the country's most accomplished chef under the age of thirty. The French Culinary Institute, his alma mater, honored him in 1993 with its first-ever Outstanding Graduate Award, praising him as one of the school's most accomplished alumni.

In May 1993, Bobby was voted the James Beard Foundation's Rising Star Chef of the Year.

Bobby Flay was awarded a presigious James Beard award for being a rising star in the culinary world. James Beard was a cooking teacher and cookbook author. The awards given in his name were established in 1990.

Bobby Flay on
⭐ Cooking for Himself

Unlike many chefs, who are so burned out from cooking at work that they go home and eat cold cereal, Bobby Flay also loves to cook at home.

His Favorite Way to Cook at Home

"I love cooking in my apartment. I love having the football game on in the background, and cooking a very slow-cooked meal so the house smells good all day long, and then by seven o'clock, you're opening a bottle of wine, putting the food on the table, finishing dinner," Flay said in a short biographical film on Biography. com.[4]

His Ultimate Dining Companion

He said on the website delish.com that if he were to have one famous person to his house to eat it would be Mohammad Ali. He said that because Ali is from Louisville, Kentucky, he would make him bourbon-glazed pork chops, cheesy grits, buttermilk biscuits, and whatever else the Champ wanted.[5]

His Favorite Meal

Thanksgiving. "I average around thirty people for dinner — friends, family, and friends of friends who can't make it home to their families. We eat, drink, laugh, watch football, play pool and Trivial Pursuit, and then eat some more. I look forward to it every year."[6]

Just two years after opening Mesa Grill, Flay tried his hand at Spanish cuisine with his restaurant Bolo. Bolo was located a few blocks from Mesa Grill, so he was able to manage both eateries.

Olé! Bold Flavors from Spain

Not only were Bobby's flavors on fire, he was on fire and in demand. Flay followed the motto of striking while iron was hot, so he and his business partner Kretchmer decided to open a second restaurant. In November 1993, they unveiled a Spanish eatery called Bolo in the Flatiron district on 22nd Street. Flay felt that New Yorkers did not really understand authentic Spanish cuisine. He had traveled to Spain to study the ingredients and preparation of Spanish food. True Spanish food, however, relied heavily on pork and animal fat, and Chef Flay believed that U.S. diners would find these fats to be too heavy and not to their liking. He modified the traditional dishes, giving them his own twist and making sure they were lighter when it came to fat content.

At Bolo, the flavor profile was far from the Southwest, but it was just as big and bold. Fried squid came with a lemony parsley pesto and an anchovy vinaigrette. Baby clams were steamed in green onion broth spiked with garlic. Eggplant was baked, presented with Manchego cheese and glazed with balsamic vinegar. The salivating crowds were downing pork loin with apples and pomegranate as well as grilled quail brushed with honey and sherry vinegar. Flay topped black squid ink pasta with sea scallops and a sauce of saffron and yellow peppers. Diners not only enjoyed the food, they loved the atmosphere as well—the room was bold, bright, and filled with energy.

Located just blocks away from the Mesa Grill, Bolo was also a critical smash with The *New York Times*, which awarded it two stars. Ruth Reichl said that somehow the venture captured the spirit of Barcelona. "Bolo vibrates with the humorous edginess of Spain's most interesting city," she wrote.[3] The Zagat Survey

Famed food critic Ruth Reichl praised Flay's cooking at both Mesa Grill and Bolo. Reichl believed Flay was creating exciting new flavor profiles for lucky New Yorkers.

voted it the best Spanish restaurant in New York City several times.

Growing Pains

Over the years, other eateries started to serve Southwestern cuisine. The craze for the food began to dim, but the Mesa Grill maintained its crowds and high rating. But in 2008, Flay felt like he got a black eye when The *New York Times* restaurant critic Frank Bruni took away one of his stars. By this time, Flay had opened several restaurants and written several books. The critic still had praise for Flay's cooking but said it was losing its excitement and becoming overly familiar, and the restaurant was churning out some inconsistent dishes. Flay has called this review by Bruni one of the low points of his career. "I think he just thought I took my eye off it," said Flay in an interview in *Inc.* "It puts you in your place—very quickly. I still feel like there's a piece of my body out there missing somewhere."[7]

> *"I still feel like there's a piece of my body out there missing somewhere."*

Still, one slightly negative review was not going to stop Flay. He kept his original restaurant going—until the New York City real estate market prevented him from going on. He could not continue Mesa Grill with soaring rents. In 2013, the landlord for the building that housed the Mesa Grill quadrupled the rent. The finances would not work. Flay was forced to close. He was very sad to lose his baby. He compared the restaurant business to Broadway shows—some have long runs and some have short runs. In terms of the restaurant business, the Mesa Grill had a solid run of 22 years.

Chapter

4

Food Becomes a
TV Star

n 1993, just as Bobby Flay was hitting his stride and getting attention in Manhattan for his bold new cooking, a new
business was starting that would change the landscape of the
food industry. That year the Food Network launched from New
York City Studios and ushered in the era of the celebrity chef.
Originally called the TV Food Network, the idea was to offer a
cable television station that would present shows about cooking, restaurants and food around the clock—twenty-four hours
a day, seven days a week. The programming on the network
divides up into in-the-kitchen programs, which are basically
instructional, how-to-cook shows that are broadcast mostly in
the day, and entertainment-related programs, such as cooking
competition shows and those related to food and travel, which
air at night.

The people who founded the station liked food but it
wasn't their driving passion. Their main interest was to provide
entertainment that viewers would keep returning to. They
wanted to sell advertisements and make money. The Food

Network wouldn't be an overnight smash. It took ten years for the channel to turn a profit.

When Bobby Flay first heard of the idea of a twenty-four hour food channel, he thought it was crazy. He didn't think there was enough content to fill all that time. Before Food Network came along, there were just a handful of chefs that really had celebrity status—Julia Child and Wolfgang Puck, for example. Food Network started with a few names who grew to be stars in the food world—Emeril Lagasse and Jacques Pepin, for example. The channel acquired the rights to Julia Child's programs that had been broadcast on public television. Most new shows were cooking demonstrations, taped all the way through without breaks or editing.

Just like when MTV first started, a lot of people didn't get it. Flay said the channel didn't have much money in the beginning. They could not afford to fly chefs in. They wanted the chefs who could appear for the cost of a subway ride. While the channel wasn't paying the chefs much at the beginning, the chefs were getting publicity and reaching a steadily growing TV audience. Flay said that some fellow chefs didn't get how to use it to their advantage. Some thought it was almost beneath them. No serious chef goes on TV—he or she stays in the kitchen. There were some who thought the whole thing would be a passing fad and that appearing on TV could damage their reputation. But Flay knew that he could get on the air, notify people that he had a restaurant, and help fill seats at the Mesa Grill and elsewhere.

Two New Loves: The Camera and a Cohost

In 1994, Flay got a call to appear on TV host Robin Leach's Food Network show, Talking Food. He knew it would be a great chance to publicize his eatery. When Leach's producers set the filming date in January 1995, Flay came running.[1]

Going on Leach's show would be the start of Flay's career as a food celebrity, but it was also momentous in another way. Leach had a co-host, the young and attractive Robin "Kate" Connelly. By this time, Flay had already divorced his first wife, Debra Ponzek, after just one and half years of marriage. Maybe their busy lives as popular chefs could not sustain a marriage. It seems that Flay and Ponzek may have remained friendly—or at least friendly on a professional level. In 2013, when Ponzek published her book The Dinnertime Survival Cookbook, it was promoted using a quote directly from Flay: "I love when talented chefs show us a little behind-the-scenes glimpse of their family meals. Debra Ponzek is the perfect chef to guide you through the rough-and-tumble chore of feeding your household."[2]

After his first appearance on Talking Food, Flay was invited back several times. He would often demonstrate how to cook a dish and his helper on-screen was usually Connelly. Flay was smitten with Connelly, who was a single mother with a young son named Jonathan. On their first date, Flay took Connelly to the world famous Monkey Bar in Manhattan. She told her babysitter that she'd be out for two hours tops.

"I got home four and a half hours later. I've never had such a good time in my life on a date, ever, ever, ever. I don't remember what I ate. There was always something to talk about. He was funny. It was the easiest thing in the world," Connelly said in the couple's New York Times wedding announcement.[3]

Flay said that he was head-over-heels for her. He was impressed that she was a career women balancing life as a single mother with an eight-year-old son. Being the fast mover that he is, Flay proposed to Connelly within a few months. In October

1995, they were married at his restaurant Bolo, and dishes from both Bolo and Mesa Grill were served.

Flay in the the *New York Times* wedding announcement admitted that the relationship might be challenging: "It's a complicated situation and the odds are against us, but that's what's great about it. If there's no challenge, why do it?"[4] By the spring following their wedding, the couple announced the birth of their daughter Sophie. Sadly, the union didn't last long. By 1998, three years after their marriage, the couple had split.

The Food Network introduced a new show called Chef du Jour in the late 1990s. A chef was invited in and would shoot five shows over the course of two days. One of Flay's chef buddies was already doing well from the show: Mario Batali. Batali owned the Italian restaurant Po in Greenwich Village. With his signature orange Crocs on his feet, the Seattle native is a big, gregarious guy full of life, humor, and stories. He knew how to charm diners who came to his restaurant and that charm translated to television and the TV audience. When he prepared food on television, he enlivened the show with facts about history, language, and culture. The Food Network liked what they saw and they gave Mario his own show called Molto Mario. Other chefs were dipping their toes into these new TV waters and they were slowly gaining notice. Flay did Chef du Jour as well. It was basically an audition to see if a chef had what it takes to be on television.

Grillin' and Chillin'

Flay started to put together a file of TV show ideas; most focused on something he knew really well: grilling. He submitted his ideas and then received a call to meet with a Food Network executive. He sat down to the meeting expecting to talk about

Flay married second wife Kate Connelly after a whirlwind romance. Although the marriage didn't last, it produced daughter Sophie, pictured here with her father.

Almost by accident, *Iron Chef* became a big hit for the Food Network. After airing English-dubbed original episodes from Japan, the network began to produce its own version, with Flay and Mario Batali (middle) as two of the Iron Chefs.

his ideas, but the network had its own plan. They wanted to pair Bobby Flay with a chef who hailed from Virginia named Jack McDavid. McDavid represented the South with a country boy vibe and Flay represented the North with a more slick and tough city attitude. Although from Virginia, McDavid's restaurants were in Philadelphia. McDavid trained in classical French cuisine, but he turned to cooking more traditional American foods and came up with "upcountry" or "haute country" dishes.

McDavid became known for his biscuits and gravy, scrapple, blueberry pancakes, Granny's meatloaf, and house-smoked pork chops and pork ribs, but all with his own touch. His two restaurants are called Down Home Diner and Jack's Firehouse. Jack wore denim bib overalls and was known for his cap that read "Save the Farm." As McDavid has said about himself, "If you don't know Jack, you don't know barbecue." McDavid liked grilling with charcoal. Flay would usually choose gas grilling. When Flay first met McDavid, he handed Bobby what he thought was beer. Bobby took a sip and nearly choked. It was moonshine.

The two got along fine, so Flay was open to the idea of partnering with McDavid. But he wanted to make sure the show went beyond just cooking up hamburgers and hot dogs. He saw that grilling could be a bit more of an art. There was more sophistication in grilling than most people think. The TV executives, Flay, and McDavid all agreed to move ahead with the program. And so the TV show *Grillin' and Chillin'* was born.

Another plus for the show: They would actually be able to shoot outside and use a real grill. In the past, many of the Food Network shows that talked about grilling were filmed indoors in the studio. So the TV host would give tips about grilling, but he couldn't actually grill. This would let them show the real deal by using an outdoor space in Florida.

At this stage, Food Network was not the powerhouse that it is today. The network didn't have the budget to pay big stars, and Flay and McDavid were not big celebrities at all except in their small local circles. They had an incredibly small budget— just $1,800 for each episode. Flay and McDavid each were paid $200 per episode. In just seven days, they filmed a whopping 42 episodes. That was six episodes per day. In Florida, they had bought grills and tables and other items needed to film. As soon as the shoot was over, the Food Network auctioned off

Jack McDavid's (left) barbecue prowess and southern country sass was a perfect counter to Flay's big city restaurant vibe. The Food Network wisely paired the two for a popular show about grilling.

everything. After the show premiered in spring of 1996, Flay noticed that his restaurant business was ticking up, and some folks were saying that they came in because they had seen him on the Food Network.

Flay and McDavid would make dishes such as pork ribs in a smoked dry rub. They brought the heat with seasoning that included ancho chile powder and jalapeños. The two would do some friendly sparring between the Northern and

Southern grilling styles. One fan of the program recalled an episode where the duo grilled tuna steaks to make tuna burgers. McDavid commented on how good the texture and color of the tuna steaks looked. Flay said, "Yeah, it's almost as red as your neck." McDavid would shoot right back, calling Flay the "city boy." He would tease Flay that he was a "city slicker" with his gas grill, and he depended on sauces to give his food taste. McDavid claimed his slow-cooking on a charcoal grill didn't need any help from an overbearing sauce to give his meat lots of flavor.

The show had many fans and was repeated often. It also solidified Flay's image and reputation as a grill master. Grilling was not Flay's only culinary talent, but it is a form of cooking he truly loves. He thinks it takes the formality out of cooking and can get everyone involved. The smells are terrific and it's a type of cooking that many men embrace and feel comfortable with.

Polishing His Act

Flay thought he had a good chance to do more. He pitched many show ideas but they seemed to be falling on deaf ears at first. Flay was determined to get more airtime. Meanwhile, Richie Jackson, a young talent agent, was noticing the rise of the celebrity-chef phenomenon. He saw that chefs like Mario Batali and Tom Colicchio (who would go on to host the long-running cooking competition Top Chef) had star potential. A new era was being born where top chefs were just as much celebrities as movie actors. Jackson approached Flay and told him he'd like to work together. Flay told Jackson about his struggles with the Food Network. Jackson said that if Food Network wasn't budging, there were other channels that might have him.

Flay was just eager to get back in front of the camera and push his restaurants.

Jackson struck a deal with the Lifetime Network, and soon Flay was back in the TV game preparing for a new show where he would be the sole host and star: *The Main Ingredient With Bobby Flay*. While Flay was good on TV, he wasn't exactly a polished or natural performer. He spoke too fast and sometimes seemed cold. Lifetime put Flay through TV training with a coach, Lou Ekus, so he would appear more likeable on camera. Ekus built a thriving business on teaching food celebrities how to articulate to an audience what was second nature to them. After all, chefs are most accustomed to being in the kitchen not in the spotlight.

When you watch chefs on television, it can seem so easy and natural, but it often takes a lot of training. TV chefs need to know how to break down their recipes for TV-friendly presentation. They need to understand the interview process and how to take control of it and use it to their advantage. They need to feel comfortable in a studio and comfortable talking while cooking—it's not as easy as you might think. Talking directly into a camera can seem unnatural at first too, and people on TV often have to read from a teleprompter so they seem like they're speaking naturally, but they're actually reading. You have to know how to carry a whole show on your own and how to bring out the best in guests. The fine art of being natural and engaging on TV is harder than it sounds, and Bobby Flay needed help.

Ekus advised Flay to basically act like he was trying to impress a date as he spoke in to the camera. He wanted Flay to act almost as if he were flirting with the camera.

Try Your Own
 # Cooking on the Internet

Lou Ekus, who helps aspiring TV chefs get camera-ready, advises young people who have aspirations to be chefs to try and present segments of themselves cooking and talking about food on the Internet. By filming food segments and posting them on the Internet, young people can realize they are really good at this. The Internet is a tool that people can use to see what they can do on camera. It's like a demo reel. Hannah Hart is a young woman who was recently discovered because of her YouTube cooking videos.

On *The Main Ingredient,* cameras followed Flay in his kitchen as he showed audiences how to prepare a range of dishes. The chef demonstrated step-by-step how to make some of his most famous meals. He also revealed some of the best places to eat while traveling. Each episode would open with cooking instructions on some of his signature barbecue dishes, such as grilled halibut with corn-coconut curry sauce, accompanied by grilled cherry tomato chutney and cucumber raita.

During the season, Flay took smaller trips to places like New York's Italian restaurant, La Puglia Ristorante, which has been around since the turn of the century. When in Mexico, the chef introduced audiences to grilled warm potato salad with roasted garlic and black olive dressing, and key lime tequila milkshake.

Famous folks would occasionally drop in on the show, such as the actors Tony Lo Bianco and Robert Woods.

Flay understood something many of his fellow chefs didn't at that time, that promoting himself on TV was a way to also promote his restaurants. His success convinced many of the early naysayers. "All those chefs have sent in their tapes since then," he told *Inc.* It makes perfect sense to market who you are and what you're doing. Honestly, I still don't think I'm very good at it. I don't practice; I'm not acting. I just try to be myself as much as possible. Sometimes I'm good at being myself and sometimes I'm not."[5]

> *"Honestly, I still don't think I'm very good at it. I don't practice; I'm not acting. I just try to be myself as much as possible."*

But Flay got better and better and he liked what TV could do beyond publicity. "I love that you're able to reach lots of people and teach, whether it's a small little tip or a full meal or somewhere in the middle," he said in a *Food & Wine* interview. "I think it's good to be able to inspire people to cook food like you do."[6]

As Flay's shows aired on Lifetime, the Food Network took notice. He was getting better at appearing on TV, although some still criticized him for speaking too fast. Flay recognized that he was a fast talker and admitted that he could be really hyper. Flay vowed that people would see the real, more relaxed Flay in his next TV show.

Television coach Lou Ekus (left) helped Bobby Flay with his on-camera presentation. While Flay is a natural talker and loves to discuss food, at first he had trouble articulating his process to an audience.

Hosting a TV Party

Flay's show would be called *Hot Off the Grill*. The executives at the Food Network, however, didn't think he could hold a show on his own yet so they paired him with Jacqui Malouf. Malouf was a Canadian comedian who had also done some hosting on TV. The concept of the show was simple. The duo would entertain friends and neighbors at indoor and outdoor celebrations in their television "home." Malouf served the role of the chipper hostess, and Flay prepared the dishes. Some saw Malouf's fun-loving perkiness as a balance to Flay's attitude, which could

> "*Watching Bobby Flay cook is fun— rapid-fire, graceful.*"

be perceived as arrogant or smug. Others simply said that Flay was knowledgeable and forceful and people misinterpreted that. Flay and Malouf worked in front of a small studio audience of usually very attractive people sitting on sofas and comfy easy chairs. The audience drank wine and laughed along like they were at a fun dinner party. The show aired every weeknight at 8:30, just before the hit show *Emeril Live* came on at 9 p.m.

To give the show some star power, they brought on celebrities such as comedians David Brenner and Todd Barry, political strategist James Carville, and Bruce Springsteen's drummer, Max Weinberg. TV audiences liked what they saw. This wasn't just a boring how-to-cook show.

In the *New York Observer*, Peter Bogdanovich praised Flay: "Watching Bobby Flay cook is fun—rapid-fire, graceful, with the economy of movement of a good cabdriver, or the cart guy who gets your coffee in three swift moves." Flay told Bogdanovich in an interview that he was successful because he knows "how to feed New Yorkers. ... When you walk into our restaurants, we want your blood pressure to go up a little." "People want to be excited, they want big-flavored food; it's got to be an event."[7]

So, Flay continued to build his reputation as the city guy who knew how to build a party with bold flavors—often around a grill.

Chapter
5

Entering the
Arena of Iron Chef

ron Chef was a television program that started in Japan in 1993 and became hugely popular there. Produced by Fuji Television, the show took place in a studio that was dubbed Kitchen Stadium. Each episode would begin with the extravagantly dressed Chairman Kaga Takeshi, whom some compared to a Japanese Liberace. He started each show by biting into a yellow pepper with great passion and he'd smile with anticipation, surveying the kitchen "battlefield" where the competition would take place.

The show had a fantastical storyline: the Chairman had spent his fortune to create Kitchen Stadium, a giant cooking arena. He wanted to encounter original cuisines that could be called true artistic creations. To realize his dream, he chose the top chefs of various styles of cooking and named his men the *Iron Chefs*—the invincible men of culinary skills. There was *Iron Chef Chinese*, *Iron Chef Japanese*, *Iron Chef French*, and *Iron Chef Italian*. At the beginning of each episode, they would appear on a platform that rose from the shadows as sweeping operatic music played.

Master chefs from all over the world would walk into the arena, past the blazing torches, and prepare to do culinary battle with one of these Iron Chefs. The atmosphere and costuming made the chefs seem like mighty super heroes. Chairman Kaga presided, watching carefully over this strange universe as the cooking gladiators did battle. They would be given a single-theme ingredient for the program and have one hour to feature that ingredient in each of their dishes in a four- or five-course meal. When the Chairman whips aside the sheet and reveals the secret ingredient, he yells out his signature call, "Allez cuisine!" That basically meant, "Start cooking!" and the competition begins.

Throughout, commentators would give their play-by-play of the cooking action and analysis of the chefs and the dishes they were making.

A wide range of ingredients have been featured, including bell pepper, strawberry, pork belly, crab, caviar, apples, lobster, egg, eel, and live squid. They even featured alligator, ostrich, and stingray. On one particularly memorable show, chefs struggled to combine soft-shell turtle with bananas. A panel of judges would rate the dishes at the end and vote on the chef they thought should be the winner.

America Embraces Cooking Campiness

For American audiences, the show was definitely odd, exotic, and fascinating because of its foreignness. *Iron Chef* originally aired in the United States in the mid 1990s on various Asian channels. It was a hit with college students and men, perhaps because the show elevated cooking to a sporting spectacle like

The original *Iron Chef*, produced in Japan, became a huge hit when it aired in the United States. Audiences delighted in the campiness of the competition, and they were fascinated by the beautiful and complex food being cooked.

professional wrestling. In 1999, the Food Network eventually began to air episodes dubbed in English, and the results were unexpectedly campy. Some compared the dubbing to watching the old monster movie *Godzilla*. In just one year, from 1998 to 1999, Food Network viewership rose about 67 percent, and many say that it was due in large part to *Iron Chef*.

Flay Raises the Roof

Iron Chef led to a crazy moment for Bobby Flay. In 1999, Fuji Television, the producers of *Iron Chef*, called the Food Network

What Is Bobby Flay's
★ Signature Dish?

Although it is almost impossible to choose one signature Bobby Flay dish, he did single out his shrimp tamales as one of his most memorable creations. This dish was at Mesa Grill from the day it opened until the day it closed. It was shrimp and roasted garlic in a fresh corn masa. He took the idea of a tamale, which started in Mexico but crossed the border into the Southwest of America, and instead of using dried corn he used fresh corn. Instead of using lard, he used butter. He made a sauce with roasted garlic and cilantro. He felt he had created the New Yorker's version of this dish.

looking for Flay. They were looking for a chef from America who could best represent the country—a rising culinary star. They wanted to bring Kitchen Stadium to the United States and have Flay do battle. Flay was the right man for the job. He was already a huge fan of the show. When he came home early in the morning after a long day of cooking, he would often unwind by watching *Iron Chef*. Plus, Flay was a born competitor. He liked to play games, and he played to win.

Flay called Fuji. He said he was in. Fuji flew its elaborate show to New York and made arrangements to set up in Webster Hall, downtown. Four Iron Chefs were coming but Flay knew he would be going up against *Iron Chef Japan*, Masaharu Morimoto.

Morimoto was a winning Iron Chef. Many remembered him for a very strong-smelling rice dish he once created that made just about everyone in Kitchen Stadium grimace. When the chefs and crews arrived, they visited Mesa Grill, enjoyed Flay's food, and asked many questions about ingredients and preparation. By all accounts, the crew from Japan were excited to be in New York City and they were a rowdy bunch.

In spring of 2000, on the night of the big battle, everything was in place. The Chairman chomped into his yellow pepper. The other Iron Chefs were on hand. The smoke poured and dramatic music rose. The crowd was yelling out in support of either Flay or Morimoto. From the ceiling, the secret ingredient for the night came down in a disco ball. It was rock crab. Flay was so pumped up with nervous energy that he accidentally put his hand in a food processor that was not turned on and cut himself on a blade. He wrapped his hand in a towel and plowed ahead. As the contest sped along, some sinks leaked water onto the floor and wires and cables were running through the water. Flay felt a shot of electricity when he touched one of the tables. Some of his helpers thought they should call off the competition, but Flay wasn't going to have it. They were going to push on and complete this thing.

As the final three seconds were counted down, Flay had an assistant help him up to stand on his cooking board. He pumped his fists in the air as if he had won. He yelled at the screaming crowd, "Raise the roof, yo!" When the announcer came to interview Morimoto after the battle, he was upset. He told the reporter about Flay, "He's not a chef. After finishing, he stood up on the cutting board. That's not right. Cutting boards and knives are sacred to us."

It was a big opportunity for Bobby Flay when he was called upon to challenge Chef Morimoto for the first-ever *Iron Chef* challenge in the United States. Flay's performance was deemed controversial, to say the least.

Morimoto offered five dishes. There was crab brain dip with bonito broth that looked like a fondue, served with udon noodles and vegetables. Crab rice came in a sour soup. Crab hors d'oeuvres were presented in two flavors—crab claw meat stir-fried in bean paste and crab and asparagus with mint. Rock crabs were grilled in seaweed with a ginger based sauce, and Japanese crab salad was prepared with citrus and pepper sauce. Bobby Flay had four dishes: crab and scallops in a coriander sauce with squid ink pasta, rock crab salad served in a coconut bowl with avocado; ethnic crab cake; and a spicy saffron soup.

> *"He's not a chef. After finishing, he stood up on the cutting board. That's not right."*

The judges unanimously voted for Morimoto, and Flay lost. Even though Morimoto won, many in Japan were outraged at the disrespect Flay showed by putting his dirty feet on the cutting board. Many agreed with Morimoto that no respectable chef would do such a thing. Bobby did it to be a showman, in the spirit of the boasting and bravado that is so common in sports.

The incident was perfect for the Food Network, however. It provided a drama and storyline that the press ate up, so to speak. Unfortunately, most stories in the press cast Flay as the bad guy—the brash, loud-mouth American who had no real respect for cooking. But Flay was just trying to join in the spirit of the show, which was really about showmanship and spectacle after all. The New York Post, the New York Times, Time, Newsweek, CNN, and other major media covered the story.

Now millions of people were aware of the Food Network and Flay helped put it on the map, and that made Flay an even a bigger star. An executive at the network told Bobby that he basically took one for the team, and the team was appreciative.

The *Iron Chef* Fuse Was Lit

Flay and his team thought that might be the end of his competing on *Iron Chef*. After all, he seemed to have angered many people with his posing atop the cutting board. But a short time after the battle aired, Fuji Television called and asked if he'd like to do a rematch in Japan. Ever the competitor, Flay agreed almost immediately. He asked for six first-class tickets to Japan. In the fall of 2000, Flay and his crew landed in Japan, seeking revenge. This second round was billed as a grudge match and a second chance for Flay to show he could beat Masaharu Morimoto.

In Kitchen Stadium, they unveiled the secret ingredient—$10,000 worth of Japanese lobster. After the Chairman entered on a white horse, Flay rose from the ground with his signature hand gesture of "raise the roof." The competition was called the Tango in Tokyo. The two chefs started with a friendly slap of the hands. Morimoto said to just have fun with this reunion.

Flay brought his American Southwestern touch—chopping corn off the cob and using corn husks, whipping up a combination of mustard, honey and horseradish, and lobster tails breaded in blue cornmeal. Toward the end, Flay threw his cutting board on the floor and jumped on the counter, giving his raise the roof hand signals. Morimoto was still disgusted, saying that standing on the cutting table was unprofessional. He stood where a chef chops food. But Morimoto said he still liked Flay.

Flay offered five dishes: a spicy marinated lobster dish with coconut and chile oil, lobster fruit salad using pomegranates and mangoes, a boiled lobster tamale in a corn husk, lobster battered in blue cornmeal, and surf and turf with kobe beef with horseradish, mustard, mint, and honey.

Morimoto offered four dishes: grilled drunken lobsters that had been soaked in sake, an appetizer with three items featuring white truffles, caviar and soft roe sauce, deep fried sushi rolls with a gorgonzola dipping sauce, and bouillabaisse shabu shabu. This time, Flay won, in a decisive four to one vote.

Iron Chef was part of shifting landscape in food television. Cooking shows had all been about dumping ingredients into a bowl, stirring, and explaining what was being cooked. A competitive show like *Iron Chef* upped the entertainment element. The show might be less about actual cooking the home audience could use, but it was more dramatic and fun, and the TV-viewing audience seemed to want that. By 2000, *Iron Chef* was beating out Emeril Lagasse's *Emeril Live* as the most-watched show on the network. Emeril brought in an average of 335,000 viewers per show versus the *Iron Chef*'s 372,000.

Flay was now a star, but by being on *Iron Chef* he was actually disrupting his own TV foundation. The Food Network now saw the entertainment value of shows like *Iron Chef* and they saw Flay's show *Hot Off the Grill* as a basic how-to show with a bit of talk, and they thought it would be better to move it to daytime rather than keep it in its nighttime slot. Flay appreciated that management was talking to him honestly about the decisions. He was basically part of the Food Network family.

When celebrity chef and host Rachael Ray was just coming along, the Food Network called on Flay to get his take on her. He watched her for twenty minutes and he knew in that short amount of time that she had something special. She had that special ingredient: she was good at being herself in front of the

Once he had established himself at the Food Network, Flay weighed in on future personalities, including Rachael Ray, who went on to tremendous success. Here, he presents her with an Emmy Award.

camera. She was natural. Flay also gave his approval of another new potential food star, caterer and personal chef Giada De Laurentiis. Flay said Giada was not only attractive but savvy about food and the entertainment business.

He appreciated his day show and doing *Iron Chef,* but he was scrambling now to create a program that would bring him back into prime time.

Americanizing the Japanese Hit

The Food Network knew they could get some mileage out of showing the dubbed Japanese *Iron Chef*, but the Japanese production team had officially ended the series in 1999. Flay and Morimoto's battle was one of a few special programs. So there would be no new content coming.

The Food Network decided to air its own version of *Iron Chef.* The producers agreed that the sheer spectacle of the show had to be maintained. They drew up plans to build an extravagant Kitchen Stadium America. The best state-of-the-art appliances were built into the design and the best kitchen tools, plates, pots, pans, etc. were bought to equip it. Carpenters, plumbers, pipe fitters, and electricians all played a vital role in building the kitchen. Bobby Flay played a crucial role in planning the show—often deciding on who would battle whom.

When *Iron Chef America: A Battle of the Masters* hit the airwaves in the spring of 2004, it was a ratings smash. In the very first episode of this American version, Flay took on the original *Iron Chef French*, Hiroyuki Sakai. Chef Sakai made his mark that episode by making trout ice cream. Sakai had the most wins of all the Iron Chefs with an 83-7 record on *Iron Chef* and 41 years of French cuisine under his apron. In this first battle, however, Flay won.

Another chef who received Flay's approval was Giada De Laurentiis, who had worked as a private chef and caterer in Los Angeles. They are now two of the faces of the Food Network.

Flay assembled California cuisine grand master Wolfgang Puck and Italian gourmet Mario Batali as his first Iron Chefs. Later, other Iron Chefs were brought on board, including Cleveland's Michael Symon and New York's Cat Cora, who both specialize in Greek and Mediterranean food, and New York's Marc Forgione and Massachusetts's Geoffrey Zakarian, who both focus on Modern Amercan cuisine. Cat Cora became the first female Iron Chef. Most of the chefs who went into the arena prepared extensively. Rick Bayless, the chef at Frontera Grill and Topolobampo in Chicago, said that he drilled his team of sous chefs for weeks before coming on the show. In the *New York Times*, he said, "We trained like we were going into the Olympics."[1]

As the series went on, *Iron Chef* experimented with pitting teams against each other. For example, Morimoto and Flay teamed up against Sakai and Batali. In 2010, Iron Chef Mario Batali and super chef Emeril Lagasse fought against Iron Chef Bobby Flay and White House Executive Chef Cristeta Comerford in a show that used ingredients from the White House garden. First Lady Michelle Obama made a special appearance. The first-prize winnings of $25,000 were donated to City Meals, a program to help feed those in need. Flay and Comerford took the prize. In a memorable 2011 episode, each dish had to have a frozen component. Flay once took on the biggest component ever—elk.

In 2007, the Food Network aired a new show called *The Next Iron Chef*. Professional chefs competed against one another in a series of elimination contests. Chef Michael Symon won the first series to become the Next Iron Chef. Flay led the panel of judges, and *The Next Iron Chef* series proved popular with audiences as the show brought more Iron Chefs into its ranks. As a judge, some find Flay intimidating—perhaps because he's won more than forty *Iron Chef* battles. Food writer Simon Majumdar has written that Flay is the most intimidating judge with his calm penetrating stare.

Iron Chef also spread internationally, with *Iron Chef UK, Iron Chef Australia*, and *Iron Chef Vietnam*. The show grew to such

Celebrity chef Alton Brown rose to fame with his show *Good Eats*. His rapidfire delivery and extensive cooking knowledge serve him well as the color commentator on *Iron Chef.*

popularity that a game for Nintendo Wii was developed based on the show. The game, *Iron Chef America: Supreme Cuisine* let players square off in Kitchen Stadium and battle through a series of fast-paced and intense culinary challenges as they make their way to the final battle for the title of *Iron Chef America*. Using game controls, players slice, chop, mix, and grate. Unfortunately, reviews of the games have been less than enthusiastic. A red-headed character looked remarkably like a cartoon version of Flay. When it comes to cooking, however, a game was no substitute for the real thing.

> *"It's just go-go-go, nonstop, so there's no forgetting anything there."*

Flay has said that being on *Iron Chef* has been his most challenging work. He doesn't like to make mistakes but because of the time pressure of *Iron Chef*, mistakes can happen. He recalled one time that he burnt some chutney. "You just lose sight of it," said Flay in *Food & Wine*. "You're trying to cook all this food in sixty minutes. I think *Iron Chef* is probably the most challenging: In sixty minutes it's just go-go-go, nonstop, so there's no forgetting anything there."[2]

Flay has made it clear several times that there's one chef in particular with whom he'd still like to battle in Kitchen Stadium. He'd like to take on the loud and provocative chef Gordon Ramsey in his kitchen. Ramsey is known for antagonizing other chefs and shouting insults at those who participate in his shows *Kitchen Nightmares* and *Hell's Kitchen*. People have asked Ramsay why he doesn't go head-to-head with Flay, and he's basically replied that he's better than that. Flay has tweeted to Ramsay: "Let's settle this like men, in the kitchen! No words, just knives. Show up or shut up."

Chapter 6

Keeping the
TV Screen Cooking

While Flay was a star through all the *Iron Chef* appearances, it really wasn't his show. It didn't put the spotlight on Flay. Flay tried other shows along the way that would highlight him as the star. He traveled the country in a program called *FoodNation with Bobby Flay*. As host, reporter, travel guide and sometime chef, he explored cities and regions across the United States, examining local culinary history and character, and meeting the people who keep these culinary traditions alive. It lasted a total of five years from 2000 to 2005, but it wasn't much of an audience grabber.

In 2002, he started filming *Boy Meets Grill*. The show was a take on a cookbook he had published in 1999 that had the same name. On the program, Flay took viewers through the grocery shopping to the grill. When the food was grilled, a lively party would often enjoy the food somewhere on location in New York City. Sometimes he would just cook in a kitchen and show the presentation. Flay barbecued up wings for a baseball team with a blue cheese yogurt dressing. For one episode, he grilled up some fish for fish tacos on a shady outdoor patio. The cookbook featured ideas to grill meats with additions such as a tarragon marinade and pineapple pecan relish.

Hunting for a Hit Show

Food Network realized that it would need to cultivate new food stars to keep its fires burning. In 2005, the network debuted *The Next Food Network Star*, which is now known simply as *Food Network Star*. Over the course of the competition series, Bobby Flay has served as judge and mentor. Alton Brown, Giada De Laurentiis, and other Food Network personalities have appeared as mentors and coaches as well. After all, it takes a unique set of skills to be able to cook, talk about food, and connect with the television audience. In this competition, contestants battle it out to get their own Food Network series. Finalists have to prove themselves in a variety of venues — food festivals, interactive media, television appearances, and various parties.

Through it all the finalists must always demonstrate the overarching theme of this competition: excellence in the kitchen, ability to share their points of view, and an on-camera presence that will attract fans and newbies alike. The show is responsible for discovering Guy Fieri, with his memorable spiky blond hair, shades, and "dude"-like attitude. Guy has gone on to host the popular *Diners, Drive-Ins and Dives*.

In 2008, Flay kept those grill fires burning when he presented *Grill It!* In this series, lucky Food Network viewers have been chosen to cook alongside the grilling guru himself in *Grill It! with Bobby Flay*. In each episode, the guest griller's best recipe is the food of the day. The twist is that Chef Flay has no clue about the food of choice until the guest arrives, so he has to whip up his own recipe on the fly. It isn't about the

As three of the Food Network's leading personalities, Flay, De Laurentiis, and Brown serve as judges on *The Next Food Network Star*.

competition. The show is really about the opportunity to grill with one of the best pit masters around.

As the savvy businessperson that he had become, Flay made sure there was a book that corresponded with the show. His book *Bobby Flay's Grill It!* was packed with the innovative marinades, sauces, vinaigrettes, and rubs.

Flay seemed to have an endless supply of shows. There was *Brunch at Bobby's*, *Worst Cooks in America*, *Bobby's Dinner Battle*, and *Beat Bobby Flay*. He also did a few one-off specials, including *Restaurant Revamp*, where he tried to help a family restaurant, and *Tasting Ireland*, where Flay returns to his ancestral land to discover its culinary treasures. He would work outside of the Food Network as well, providing cooking segments on CBS's *The Early Show* and *America's Next Great Restaurant* on NBC.

Throwdown Pushes Ratings Up

Perhaps the show that was to make the biggest impact for Flay after *Iron Chef* was called *Throwdown*. Food Network programmers were looking for something a bit more entertaining than the usual fare, and other than *Iron Chef America*, most of the shows connected with Bobby Flay were fairly straightforward. The executives at the channel wanted something with a hook—maybe some kind of unique competition. Flay listened closely and thought carefully. He looked out at the TV landscape and thought about what people like to watch.

He thought about the show *Punk'd* on MTV. It was hosted by the actor Ashton Kutcher and in

> *He looked out at the TV landscape and thought about what people like to watch.*

many ways it was like the old television show *Candid Camera*. The key ingredient in *Punk'd* was fooling a celebrity on hidden camera. If you were "punk'd," you were the victim of the prank.

First, Flay thought he could do some sort of Food Network equivalent where he pulled a gag on the top food celebrities— Emeril, Rachel Ray, etc. But he thought that was too narrow and he'd run out of big name celebrities fairly quickly. Then, he hit upon the idea of surprising top chefs in different communities around the country. The chefs would be told that they've been selected to be featured as part of a food program that would focus on their preparation of one of their specialties. Cameras from the Food Network would be set up already, so hidden cameras wouldn't be needed. Then Flay would pop up out of nowhere and say that he was challenging them to a food duel of sorts. He wanted to go head-to-head with them making his twist on their top dish—whether it be falafels, fish tacos, chili, wedding cake.

The chefs would be surprised but most likely—he thought— they would go along with the scheme since they were ready to cook any way. Part of the show would be a segment that Flay taped before the confrontation of him figuring out his dish for the competition. The chefs would cook and people who were there would eat the food and talk about it. That was his entire idea at this point. Flay loved the surprise element and thought that it would be a great hook just like on *Punk'd*. His name for the show was "*Cook'd*."

Programmers liked Flay's idea—for the most part. They did not like the name of the program and they wanted there to be a clear winner each episode. Flay thought the idea was good as is—the surprise and the food were there. He thought that that was enough to make a solid program. After about a month

In 2006, Flay started taping a new show called *Throwdown! with Bobby Flay.* This was a competition in which Flay would challenge a chef or cook to a throwdown and would try to do a better job than they did in cooking their signature dish.

of debating how the show should run, Flay agreed to changes. In the revised version, after Flay and the chef battled it out, a judge or panel of judges would have a blind taste test and choose their winner. They hashed over new names for the show and came up with *Throwdown*. The show was sold as Bobby Flay on a secret mission to challenge the best of the best.

Just like *Iron Chef* had its gimmick of being introduced by the Chairman in his Kitchen Stadium, Flay came up with his own distinct opening. Spy-like music would play and a bike messenger would catch Flay off guard and deliver a secret file about the chef who was targeted and the dish to be prepared. (Later in the series, Flay would retrieve the file from a safe or in other ways.)

The first episode aired in 2006. It featured Butch Lupinetti, owner of Butch's Smack Your Lips BBQ in Mount Laurel, New Jersey. "Barbeque to me is a 365 day-a-year job," he tells the camera. His secret to great barbecue was low and slow cooking. Lupnetti made smoky chicken, ribs, and hog and beat out a very gracious Flay. Flay wanted to give competitors every chance to win. He said if the show was about him beating all these chefs across the country, no one would like him. Flay did lose more than he won. But there were impartial judges, so Flay would occasionally take home the top prize. Flay said he didn't mind losing either because in the end the show really wasn't about winning or losing, it was about the chefs and the people.

The Food Network loved the program because it cast Bobby Flay as a friend to the people. It joined their primetime programming schedule and proved to be a great hit. Flay seemed to have the knack, will, and drive to change and adapt, and succeed on televison. The show ran through 2011.

A Third Try at Love

Throwdown and many other Flay shows would occasionally feature his third wife, actress Stephanie March. In 2010, the Food Network launched a spinoff called the Cooking Network. The focus was to be more on the cooking than the reality-based, competition-based programming. Of course, Flay would be in the mix and producers wrangled him and March into filming a show called *Brunch at Bobby's* where the couple would prepare meals at their country home in Long Island.

Viewers loved seeing the couple working together on TV. On one program, March cooked Flay's birthday dinner of filet mignon, jalapeño-cheese grits and a buttermilk-custard pie. March was appearing on *Law & Order: SVU* when she met Flay. Her costar Mariska Hargitay and one of the cameramen conspired to introduce Flay and March. Flay asked Hargitay if March might go on a date with him. At first, March gave a flat out "no." March had heard that Flay was a ladies' man who liked to date a lot. So she was reluctant at first. On the *Rachael Ray Show*, she said that the first meal he ever made her was breakfast. "He said what do you like on your toast and I said butter and honey," she said. "It was beautiful."[1] At Bar Americain, he created a brunch dish in her honor: Miss Stephanie's Biscuits and Cream Gravy with Sausage and Scrambled Eggs.

For ten years, the couple appeared to be powerful, loving, and together. As Flay appeared on more and more television shows and opened more restaurants, March acted and became involved in good causes. She traveled to Nepal and India with World of Children Award, for example, to check on a clinic for children with muscular disabilities and a clinic that rehabilitates people who are the victims of sex trafficking. She also opened a makeup salon called Rouge NY. But by spring of 2015,

Flay married actress Stephanie March, but the third time was not a charm. The two divorced in 2015.

What Does It Take to
⭐ Beat Bobby Flay

On the Food Network website, top food industry professionals give their tips on what it takes to beat Flay.

Giada De Laurentis says that there are a couple things that are not his strong points: pasta and desserts. "He brings bold flavors to the table so competitors need to bring flavors that will stand up against his."

Chef Alex Guarnaschelli advises chefs to be true to themselves. "You need a real sense of culinary identity."

Chef Geoffrey Zakarian insists he can take down Flay with one arm tied behind his back and wearing an eye patch. He advises chefs to use few ingredients and use them well. "If you try to use all the ingredients, he will kill you."

Chef Aarón Sanchez advises beating Flay at his own game: "Utilize chiles— the affinities he has toward certain ingredients and flavors. I think that's the way to beat him because then if you do better than him, it's so obvious."

Chef Jonathan Waxman, Flay's original mentor, said that it's pretty easy to bring Flay down: "Just don't get complicated."[2]

the fuzzy glow was gone and the couple was heading toward divorce.

Everyone Wants to Beat Bobby

No matter what was happening in his personal life, Flay was always pushing forward in his professional life. In 2012, Flay tried his stab at reality television with a series called *3 Days to Open*. In the series, Flay visited new restaurants that were opening three days after his arrival. He made a list of things that he thought needed to be fixed by opening night, and spent those three days preparing the owners for opening, and attempting to check every concern off his list. Restaurateurs with no prior experience in the high stakes world of food participated in the show. With everything on the line — including savings, live-lihood, and integrity — these new businesses needed Bobby's help, or failure was imminent. They all race against the clock to make sure their opening night doesn't become their closing night.

This show was a nice departure for Flay, but it didn't satisfy his need for competition. He wanted to compete more against other chefs. He recognized that as a chef who is so incredibly popular, others want the opportunity to take him down a notch. He wanted to give up-and-coming chefs a chance to come on stage and show what they got against him. That's why he came up with the show *Beat Bobby Flay* in 2013. Flay says he wanted to give people an opportunity to take him down. He says that this is sort of the street version of *Iron Chef*. The fact is, it's super hard to beat Bobby Flay. In the first season, he had ten head-to-head cooking confrontations, and he only lost two.

The show takes place in two rounds. In the first round, two chefs compete to square off against Flay. He chooses the

Bobby Flay has said that, as much as he loves to cook, he loves teaching people how to cook even more. He has reached millions of people through his television shows, and he gives cooking demonstrations at food festivals and state fairs.

ingredient and off they go to make a dish in twenty minutes. Then in round two, the winning chef battles Flay with his or her signature dish. Three experts come in and do a blind taste test and choose the winner.

Most recently, Flay put together a Food Network program called *Bobby Flay's Barbecue Addiction*. Here, Flay is back to demonstrating grilling techniques, from charcoal to smoke to gas. Some of his recipes have featured BBQ ribs with root beer BBQ sauce, beer-simmered bratwurst, and grilled skirt steak with green and smoky red chimichurri.

The fact is, it's super hard to beat Bobby Flay.

Flay has said that one of his greatest joys of being on television is that he is able to teach others how to cook and inspire them to cook.

Chapter
7

Cooking
and Beyond

Although his heart is in cooking, Flay has expanded his interests and business beyond the stovetop. Part of his website is dedicated to fitness, branded as Bobby Flay Fit. He has a seven-part web series showing how he stays fit. He talks about discipline, weightlifting, and running. He admits that the world of cooking can lead to weight gain. The restaurant business is about eating. He had been eating a lot more and indulging in more late-night meals, but he's cut back on that.

Flay doesn't offer any diet plans, or have a list of must-dos or never-eats. He believes in eating EVERYTHING in moderation. He also believes in challenging himself daily with a variety of different workouts: running, swimming, rowing, biking, yoga, even walking. His philosophy is to just keep moving and burn more calories than he consumes. He suggests exercise regimes, apps for your smart phones, the latest in workout gear, and everything that has to do with trying to lead a fit lifestyle. Naturally, healthy recipes that help keep people trim are part of the picture.

It only seemed like a natural progression that Flay would start to sell some of his unique culinary creations, packaging them for the mass market. On his website, you can see a range of sauces and rubs—steak sauces, steak rubs, poultry rub, and hot sauce. He's attached his name to cookware as well. Kohl's now produces a 320-product line of cooking-related items with Bobby Flay's name on them. The products include ceramic bakeware, grilling tools, utensils, knives, pots, pans, linens, and towels.

Flay has written more than a dozen cookbooks. His latest, *Bobby Flay's Barbecue Addiction*, includes recipes for jazzed-up hamburgers, Tuscan smoked rosemary chicken, sides, and cold drinks.

In line with his competitive spirit, Flay has another passion that he has been able to grow as he has become more successful. He now owns a thoroughbred racehorse, More Than Real. The filly was the winner of the 2010 Breeders' Cup Juvenile Fillies Turf Race. Famous jockey Garret Gomez rode her to victory. Flay sees long-term gains from buying racehorses in the fact that they can be bred and he can sell the offspring down the road. He has advised those who want to own a racehorse but don't have a lot of money to consider buying a percentage of a horse that is owned by a syndicate. This method lets a person own a percentage of a horse.

Burgers and Beyond

While Flay has been fully immersed in the Food Network and busy with these various other ventures, he ultimately does it all so he can cook for people. Restaurants are his true love, so although he devoted much of his life to creating TV, he always

Flay has expanded his business ventures beyond restaurants and into merchandising. His line of kitchenware products debuted in 2008.

wanted to be presenting his culinary creations to the dining public.

Flay opened his second Mesa Grill at Caesar's Palace in Las Vegas in 2004. That restaurant would win him a very coveted Michelin star. None of his other restaurants earned that prestigious recognition. In 2007, he would build a third Mesa Grill in the Bahamas at Atlantis Paradise Island. He also established Bobby Flay Steak in the Borgata Hotel Casino & Spa in Atlantic City, New Jersey.

To keep his restaurant empire on the rise, Flay opened Bar Americain on 52nd Street in Midtown Manhattan with his business partner Laurence Kretchmer in 2005. This restaurant is an American brasserie. (In the 1930s, *Bar Americain* was the term for a Parisian restaurant with a full bar.) The bold southern flavors were still here but *New York* magazine said that Flay was trying for a more sophisticated approach here. The room is bathed in a low orange glow and features a raw bar where shellfish are shucked and served. The *New York Times* food critic Sam Sifton liked the restaurant, declaring it fun and saying, "As Bar Americain presents and riffs on what it sees as American classics and classically American ingredients—the barbecued pork inside orange-tinged squash blossoms; the faintly orange grits beside sautéed shrimp—it strives for and achieves warm, festive, accessible effects."[1]

Bar Americain bustles along and is often a destination of theater goers. Flay opened another Café Americain with a similar look and feel at the Mohegan Sun Casino in Uncasville, Connecticut. It's one of the largest casinos in the United States.

In 2008, Flay (along with Kretchmer) wanted to try something more for the common man. Flay has always loved hamburgers. In fact, when he gets off of work and wants to

Bobby Flay has authored more than a dozen popular cookbooks for the home cook, including *Boy Meets Grill* (1999) and *Bobby Flay's Barbecue Addiction* (2013).

relax, more often than not he races to get a late-night burger. They opened their first Bobby's Burger Palace in the Smith Haven Mall in Lake Grove, New Jersey. This would be the first of a growing chain of "fast casual" restaurants under the Flay name. The count currently stands at eleven. The menu is burgers, fries, and shakes. Flay has said the eateries were a tribute to the burger joints of his youth. The restaurants sometimes feature a burger that represents that location. The LA burger has avocado relish, tomato, cheddar cheese, and watercress, while the New Mexico burger has roasted green chiles and a queso sauce. The Carolina burger has smoked American cheese, green onion slaw, and mustard barbecue sauce. The Vegas burger features pickled Fresno chiles with white American cheese and barbecue potato chips.

Flay says that one of the trademarks at his burger joints is "crunchify-ing" his patties by adding chips to any of the burgers. His Green Chile Cheeseburger won the Amstel Light People's Choice Award at the Food Network South Beach Wine and Food Festival in 2013. He also serves a Brunch Burger with a fried egg, smoked bacon, and American cheese. Flay boasts about his French fries, which he says are made fresh and not from a frozen package. Potatoes are cut, soaked overnight, then blanched in canola oil. The fries are cooked halfway through ahead of time. Then, when ordered, they are fried at 375 degrees. The milkshake menu also offers creative choices, like blueberry pomegranate and pistachio. Flay boasts that his milkshakes go the extra mile by offering eleven ounces of ice cream. Burgers are six ounces and start at $6.50. Flay is big on condiments. He likes horseradish, mustard, salsa, avocado relish, and chipotle ketchup.

Flay is pushing his patties on college campuses as well, at University of Maryland and the University of Pennsylvania. He hopes to expand the chain into more schools and created Bobby's Burger Palace University. He wants to get students involved in promoting BBP and being ambassadors. That's a system he uses at University of Maryland. Students work in the restaurants, they encourage other students to come in and they hold events.

People Behind His Success

With six fine dining restaurants, eighteen burger restaurants, and a TV production company, Flay has to be a businessman everyday. He has about 1,600 employees now. He spends a lot of his day inspiring people to do the best job that they can do. He believes there's only one way to inspire people—you have to go there and be there.

When Bobby Flay talks about his success, he credits the people who work for him with making his multi-tasking life work. He says that he could not do it without them. He has particularly relied on four women whom he calls his B Team (not that they are rated B, just that they are on the Bobby Team). His personal team is Stephanie Banyas, Sally Jackson, Christine Sanchez, and Elyse Tirrell. They help him do everything from writing his cookbooks to keeping his life on schedule.

"There are two things I look for [in hiring people]: if they're nice and if they're ambitious," he explained on the *Daily Meal* website. "I am always observing how people do their job, how they work, if they're making the customers' experiences better, if they're on time for work, all the fundamentals during every single moment in my restaurants." He also believes in the

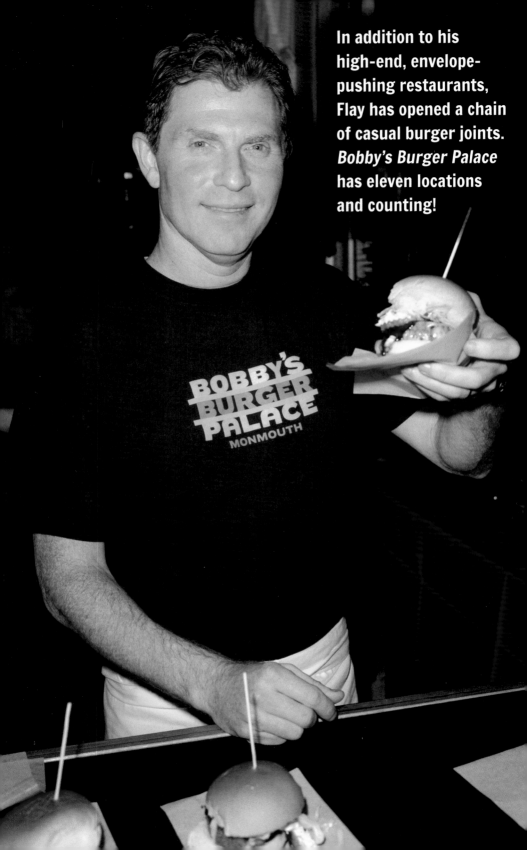

In addition to his high-end, envelope-pushing restaurants, Flay has opened a chain of casual burger joints. *Bobby's Burger Palace* has eleven locations and counting!

strength of women: "If it's up to me, I think women should exclusively rule the world."[2]

Flay continues to get inspiration from others—from eating at other's restaurants, and from traveling. Flay says that the restaurant industry may be the most generous industry in the world. "We're all competitive," Flay said on the Heritage Radio Network. "The competition is fierce but the camaraderie is even fiercer. We pass employees , sources, and recipes back and forth."[3]

Back to Basics

Early on, Flay's restaurants had earned him respect in the culinary world. In some ways, his constant barrage of TV appearances seemed to be detracting from how he was regarded as a chef. It felt as if his credibility was being questioned. Mesa Grill and Bolo had brought him that special critical attention, but in 2007 he closed Bolo when a realtor took over the space for condominiums. The developer took over the block and Bolo was yet another New York City casualty. In 2013 he was force to close Mesa Grill because of skyrocketing rents.

Flay told the *New York Times* how emotional it was to give up Mesa Grill. He served his last meal in August of 2013. His daughter was with him, and she could tell that her father was getting very upset. She told him that it was OK to cry. Flay said that this was his youth. It was his whole life. His entire career was born of the Mesa Grill and now it was closing. He let himself have a good cry.

Flay has complained that New York is just getting too expensive—even for a star like him. The high rents are making it close to impossible to have a new successful restaurant. He tweeted: "A note to NY landlords. Good restaurants are closing

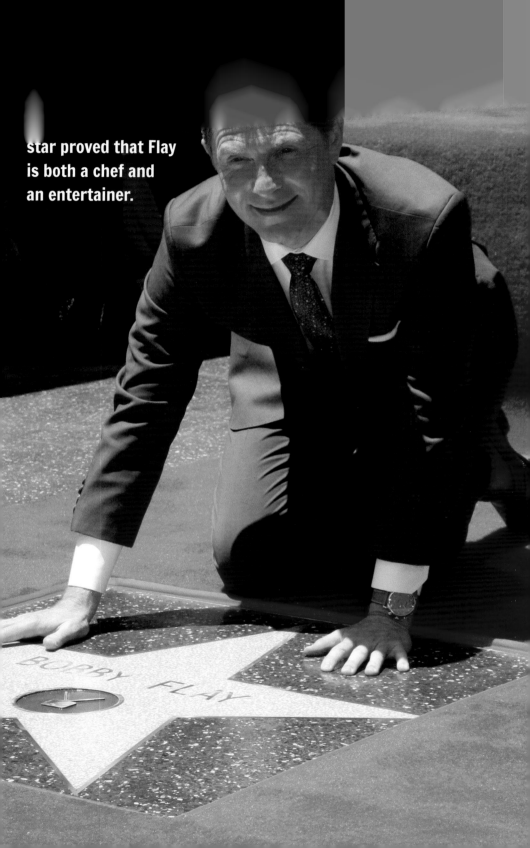

star proved that Flay is both a chef and an entertainer.

all over the city because the rents are impossible to pay. Stop turning NYC into a mall."

With Bolo and Mesa Grill shuttered, Flay did not have one restaurant where he felt he could be new and fresh. He wanted a place where he could prove that he was still an important chef who had what it takes in the kitchen.

"Food is the thing that is my life. It is the thing I like to do for work and it is the thing I like to do for pleasure," said Flay on *Chef's Story* on the Heritage Radio Network. "I always tell people that I do that same thing that I do to work that I do to relax, which is cook. I'm always going to be a chef first. The media stuff has been terrific because it was opened a lot of doors. I'm a cook first, always."[4]

Flay was driven to open a new place that would recapture the old magic. Plus, Flay is a New Yorker through-and-through, so he really wanted have another restaurant that would showcase his cooking talents. He had been on the lookout even as far back as when Bolo shuttered its doors, but now more than ever, he wanted it. He already had two Mesa Grills still cooking along. What he really wanted was something in the vein of Bolo that would let him highlight some Spanish flavors.

> *"Food is the thing that is my life. It is the thing I like to do for work and it is the thing I like to do for pleasure."*

In 2014, Flay unveiled Gato on Lafayette Street in Manhattan, just north of Houston Street. Gato expands beyond the Spanish influence to serve foods inspired by countries throughout the Mediterranean—Italy, Greece, and North Africa. Here Flay stresses olive oil, anchovies, capers, citrus, tomatoes, and hot and sweet peppers. For inspiration, he and his partner Kretchmer hopped a plane to Europe to take an intensive food tour. Flay finds great inspiration in cooking from around the world. The duo went to Paris, Rome, and Barcelona. Barcelona was especially eye-opening—or maybe taste opening. In the *New York Times*, Flay described having an amazing, transforming dish of artichokes and eggs. He said that the scrambled eggs were perfect and there was no other dish in the world he'd rather be eating. The menu at Gato now features his take on the dish.

The reviews have been favorable. The *New York Times* gave Gato two stars. The food critic Pete Wells raved about the dishes: "Mr. Flay sometimes lights up the tilt sign on his pinball machine, there is still a lot to love on the menu. There is a lot, period. Gato shows an all-too-rare generosity in its flavors, its eager service, its good-tempered desserts, like the summery blackberry crostata and the fromage blanc cheesecake whipped into a froth by the pastry chef, Clarisa Martino."[5]

The *Times* critic also liked the restaurant so much that he picked it as one of the 10 Best New Restaurants of 2014. The food critic Alan Richman gave Gato three stars. Richman was not only bowled over by the food, but he was bowled over by the fact that Flay was in the kitchen cooking. After all, this was a busy TV chef. How could he have time to be there? But lo and behold, Richman wrote: "He was pale, washed-out from too many hours in an airless, sun-starved kitchen. He was too thin, too tired. He wasn't beaming. He had actually been in the Gato kitchen all night, and he proved it by rattling off our orders, even the allergies of one friend. Bobby Flay had been cooking the food, working the line, walking the walk."[6]

Some people are inclined to think that Flay would not be able to deliver at Gato, but consistently he has been surpassing expectations. The *New York Post* restaurant critic wrote that Gato is "infuriatingly excellent."[7]

Flay has explained that TV does not have to pull him away from cooking in the restaurant. He said he can shoot an entire season of *Beat Bobby Flay* in three or four days. He just has to make sure he does costume changes in between. Flay estimates he spends 80 percent of his time in his restaurants.

While Flay always says his true passion is cooking in a restaurant, he admits that it is incredibly hard to make a profit in the restaurant business. He has said that his two highest grossing restaurants are Bobby Flay Steak in Atlantic City and Mesa Grill in Las Vegas. His burger chain does rake in millions each year, but Flay says that most gets poured back into the business. Flay has said that even if he fills all the 130 seats in Gato every night, it will be difficult to make money.

Gato seems to be filling the hole that was left after Mesa Grill and Bolo had closed. While his sadness over their loss may be lifting, he still holds such a soft spot for his for restaurant Mesa Grill that he may still bring it back. In an article on the website *Eater* in 2014, Flay said that he promised to reopen his old friend somewhere—it might be in Manhattan but it might also be in Louisville, Kentucky. As of this writing, he was still out there scouting locations.

Looking Back

Flay says the food world has changed so much since he started in the business. People today are much more interested in food than ever before. He credits Wolfgang Puck for how the

What Is Bobby Flay
★ **Really Like?**

As boisterous and loud as Bobby Flay is on television, chef and friend Michael Symon said that Flay is the opposite in real life. In an interview on the Food Network website, Symon said, "He's a pretty quiet guy. [There's] the personality they see on TV of Bobby — he's very outgoing on television, obviously — but in real life he's a pretty quiet guy. Pretty to himself, quiet guy. Very thoughtful guy." He also says he's true to himself.

"I don't do anything on TV that I don't enjoy doing. It's important to stay true to who you are, what your passions are, and how you want to be perceived," Flay said.[8]

food industry changed in this country, noting that it took an Austrian to do it.

"The guy is amazing," Flay said in his interview with Dorothy Hamilton. "He cares about the food first. The guy is like magic. I feel like every time I go to one of his restaurants, he's there and he's got millions of restaurants."

And Flay tries to follow Puck's lead. He shows up in the kitchens of his burger place in New Jersey and in Bar Americain. Before Wolfgang Puck, good food was only very high end in very quiet dining rooms, according to Flay. Puck showed that food could be good and whimsical. He took the formality out of really good eating and he was able to make a good business out of it.

In his interview with Dorothy Cann Hamilton, Flay also discussed how his food has changed over time. "I think it has gotten simpler. As time goes on, you get more confident so you need fewer bells and whistles."[9]

Flay has said that he is far from perfect. One of the things that he's proud of is that every day he lays it on the line. He's not afraid of what people are going to think. He believes that if you hold yourself back, you can never be true to yourself. Sometimes, he proceeds with what he believes and doesn't listen to anyone else. That can work out, but he has had failures as well.

When he first opened Bolo, he created a dish that he thought was going to revolutionize paella. It featured arborrio rice with lobster and duck, and lobster stock and duck stock. He was convinced it would be the dish that would make Bolo. But staff and friends tried the dish and they said it wasn't good. It just was not working. But Flay told them that they were all wrong. Ruth Reichl, the critic for the *New York Times* at the time, came in and gave a great review of Bolo, but she spent a paragraph talking about how bad this lobster-duck paella was. She was concerned for the lobster

"You need people to help you be who you are."

and hoped it would be able to crawl out of the bowl to get away. Flay said he learned his lesson. Still, he believes in the motto: No risk, no reward.

His advice to culinary students coming up: Slow growth. He thinks that every one expects instant success. "Just as I build the layers of flavors in my dishes, I build the layers of my career the same way. I tell people if you want to follow my career and

Everybody wants griling tips from Bobby Flay, even President Barack Obama! Flay and Obama grilled up some food for a mentoring event at the White House in 2009.

do what I did, learn how to cook first. Learn how to say no to things. If it's a compromise, don't do it. I always say, 'If people ask you now, they'll ask you again.' I hire people for two reasons. If they're ambitious and if they're nice. You need people to help you be who you are."[10]

Becoming a Chef

For many, the path to becoming a chef is similar to Bobby Flay's career. You have to learn the skills by doing. Work experience is the main ingredient. Many top chefs like Flay, Anthony Bourdain, Michael Mina, Grant Achatz, David Chang, and Todd English all went to culinary school. Mario Batali attended London's Le Cordon Bleu for a short time but dropped out, deciding he would learn more from great chefs who were working at top restaurants. Pro chefs Ashley Christensen, Barbara Lynch, and Susan Goin did not go to culinary school. By learning on the job, they paved their way to success.

While culinary school isn't necessary, it can provide an aspiring chef with the skills needed to enter a kitchen and perform from the get-go. Even knowing the language of cooking (names of sauces, methods of heating, etc.) can go a long way when entering a professional kitchen. Most programs cover all the bases when it comes to working in a restaurant. Beyond cooking techniques (like knife skills) and kitchen operations, culinary school courses cover menu planning, food sanitation procedures, and purchasing and inventory methods. Most training programs also require students to get real-world experience. Through connections from their schools, students may complete internships or apprenticeships in commercial kitchens. Some community colleges and technical schools also offer professional training in cooking. More than 200 academic training programs at post-secondary schools are accredited through the American Culinary Federation (ACF). The ACF also organizes certification programs—chefs that receive certification demonstrate that they have reached a certain level of competence. Students should keep in mind that cooking school can be expensive and may require paying back loans for years to come.

The Bureau of Labor Statistics lists the following talents as being important to succeeding at this job:

Business skills. Many chefs run their own business or are in charge of the finances at a restaurant. They can benefit from learning how to handle administrative tasks, such as accounting and personnel management, to be able to manage a restaurant efficiently and profitably.

Communication skills. Chefs need to be able to communicate quickly and clearly with their staff to make sure food is being executed properly and brought to the tables in an efficient manner.

Creativity. The chefs who truly shine come up with their own dishes. They take time to be creative and develop interesting and innovative recipes. They should be able to use various ingredients to create appealing meals for their customers.

Dexterity. For chefs and head cooks, their job depends on fast, clean, and precise cutting techniques. It's all in the hands—so manual dexterity is a must.

Leadership skills. Chefs need to motivate, instruct, and organize kitchen staff to get meals completed and served. Developing a cooperative atmosphere for staff is an essential skill.

Sense of taste and smell. Chefs depend on a keen sense of taste and smell, to inspect food quality and to cook meals that will have customers coming back for more.

Time-management skills. Chefs must efficiently manage their time and the time of their staff. They must ensure that meals are prepared and that customers are served in a reasonable time frame, especially during busy hours.

Chef Anthony Bourdain, who is now a TV food celebrity, shares a few other insights on what it takes to succeed as a chef in his book *Medium Raw*. He warns newbies that they have to be ready to work long hours and for low wages at first. He advises those who want to cook in the best kitchens to try and land a job or even work for free in a great kitchen. That experience on a résumé can open doors later. Time spent in a chain restaurant, hotel kitchen, or country club may pay the bills for a while, but it won't lead to being a top chef, in most cases. Cooking takes physical endurance and strength. There can be a lot of moving of trays and sacks of ingredients. There can be bending over, picking up, and stretching high. Plus, standing on your feet all day in a hot environment takes endurance—and the hours can be long.

Try It Yourself!

Fish Tacos

Serves 4

Ingredients

¼ cup (60 mL) sour cream

2 tablespoons (30 mL) lime juice

1/2 teaspoon (2.5 mL) cumin

1/2 teaspoon chili powder

salt and pepper to taste

1 jalapeño, cut lengthwise and seeded

2 ½ cups (595 mL) shredded red cabbage

4 green onions, thinly sliced

2 tablespoons olive oil

1 pound (450 g) tilapia filets (or any other sturdy white fish such as mahi mahi, cod, or monk fish), cut into strips

(8) 6-inch (15 cm) tortillas

½ cup (120 mL) fresh chopped cilantro

Directions

1.) Combine sour cream and lime juice in a large bowl. Season with salt and pepper. Keep about half the mixture in another bowl for serving.

2.) Mince half the jalapeño pepper and save the rest for later. Toss cabbage, green onions, and minced jalapeño half in remaining sour cream mixture until slaw is well mixed.

3.) In a large skillet, heat olive oil and remaining jalapeño half. Coat pan evenly.

4.) Season tilapia fillets with salt and pepper, cumin and chili powder. Pan-fry fish strips in the skillet until fish is golden brown and easily flaked with a fork (it will probably take about two batches). This should take five to six minutes for each fillet. Discard jalapeño.

5.) Heat tortillas in the microwave on high until warm, Twenty to thirty seconds.

6.) Serve fish in warm tortillas topped with cabbage slaw, reserved sour cream mixture, and cilantro.

Chicken Enchiladas

Serves 5

Ingredients

2 tbsp (30 mL) olive oil

1.5 lbs (595 g) of chicken legs/ thighs (can use breast meat, but thighs have more flavor)

1 jalapeño, with stem and seeds removed and diced

3 garlic cloves, minced

1/2 large white onion, diced

1 tsp (5 mL) chili powder

1 tsp cumin

1 cup (240 mL) fresh cilantro leaves

Juice of one lime

salt and pepper to taste

16 oz cheese: monterrey jack, cheddar, Oaxaca, or some combination of the three

(12) 6-inch (15 cm) corn tortillas

Salsa verde (tomatillo salsa)

Directions

1.) In medium saucepan, place olive oil, chicken, spices, and half the lime juice. Cover with water (about three cups) and bring to a boil. Once boiling, reduce heat to low and simmer until the chicken is tender and it easily comes apart with a fork)about thirty-five minutes).

2.) Remove chicken from pot and let rest. Dump most of the cooking liquid, saving 1/4 cup in the pot. Add vegetables, remaining lime juice, and half of the cilantro. Cook on medium heat until vegetables begin to soften (about seven-eight minutes).

3.) Using tongs to hold the chicken, carefully dice it (or simply pull it apart with a fork).

4.) Add chicken and remaining cilantro to vegetables/spices, and stir until well combined. At this time, you may add more spices, if you like things a little spicier. This mixture is your enchilada filling.

5.) Meanwhile, place the tortillas in a microwave on high about twenty-thirty seconds, or until warm to the touch. They should be soft enough to roll without breaking, but still stiff enough to hold up.

6.) Grease a 9x13-inch (23x32 cm) baking dish, and preheat oven to 400°F (205°C).

7.) Place one tortilla on a flat surface. Place approx. two tbs of chicken mixture in the center of the tortilla, spreading it in a thick line down the middle.

Top with a small handful of cheese. Gently wrap the tortilla around the chicken and cheese. Very carefully, place the enchilada, seam down, in the baking pan. Repeat until all meat is used.

8.) Cover the enchiladas with salsa verde. This is a very simple sauce made from tomatillos, cilantro, and jalapeños. You can make it yourself, or buy pre-made. Either way is fine.

9.) Once the enchiladas are saucy, cover with remaining cheese. Cover pan with aluminum foil and bake until tortillas are soft and the cheese is melted.

10.) Let sit for ten minutes before serving. Use sour cream and cilantro for garnish, if desired.

Grilled Skirt Steak With Chimichurri Sauce

Serves 4

Ingredients

For the chimichurri:

1/2 cup (120 mL) packed fresh parsley leaves

1/2 cup fresh oregano leaves

1/4 cup (60 mL) packed fresh cilantro leaves

1/4 cup extra-virgin olive oil

2 garlic cloves, finely minced

2 teaspoons (10 mL) white wine vinegar

1 tablespoon (15 mL) lime juice

1/2 teaspoon chili power

1/2 teaspoon ground cumin

1/2 teaspoon salt

1/8 teaspoon freshly ground black pepper

For the steak:

1/2 teaspoon smoked paprika

1/2 teaspoon salt

1/4 teaspoon black pepper

Ground cayenne to taste (1/8 to 1/4 teaspoon)

1 1/4 (563 g) pounds skirt steak

Directions

Preheat the broiler and coat a broiler pan with cooking spray.

For the chimichurri:

Mix the parsley, basil, cilantro, olive oil, garlic, vinegar, lime juice, coriander, cumin, salt, and pepper in a food processor until smooth.

For the steak:

1.) Combine the steak spices and sprinkle the mixture evenly over both sides of the steak.

2.) Put the steak on the prepared rack and broil 3 to 4 minutes per side for medium rare.

3.) Transfer to a cutting board and allow the meat to rest five minutes.

4.) Cut on the diagonal in 1/4-inch to 1/2-inch wide strips.

5.) Serve drizzled with the chimichurri sauce.

Grilled Pork Chops With Maple Balsamic Glaze

Serves 4

Ingredients

6 tablespoons (90 mL) maple syrup

6 tablespoons balsamic vinegar

¾ teaspoon salt

¾ teaspoon pepper

(4) 12-oz (340 g) boneless pork loin chops
    1-1/2 inches (3.5 cm) thick

Directions

1.) Whisk syrup, vinegar, salt and pepper until blended
    in a small bowl. This is your marinade.

2.) Pour 1/2 cup marinade into a large resealable plastic bag. Add pork chops. Seal bag and toss gently to coat. Refrigerate 1 hour. Keep the remaining marinade for basting later.

3.) Take pork chops from marinade and throw out used marinade and bag.

4.) Put some cooking oil on a paper towel and rub it on a cool grill rack to coat. Turn on heat.

5.) Grill pork chops, covered, over medium heat (or broil) for thirteen-seventeen minutes or until a thermometer reads 145°F (63°C), turning occasionally and basting with reserved marinade during the last five minutes.

6.) Let stand five minutes before serving.

Cheeseburger

Serves 4

Ingredients

1 pound (450 g) ground beef (20% fat)

2 tablespoons (30 mL) Worcestershire sauce

1/2 teaspoon (2.5 mL) paprika

4 teaspoons (20 mL) softened butter

4 hamburger buns, split

Coarse salt and ground pepper

4 slices melting cheese, such as American or
mild cheddar

Directions

1.) Heat broiler.

2.) In a medium bowl, combine ground beef, Worchester sauce, and spices.

3.) Divide beef into 4 rounds. Place each between two layers of plastic wrap. Flatten beef with a rolling pin and form into 1/4-inch-thick patties.

4.) Butter inside of each bun and put them on a baking sheet with buttered side up. Toast under broiler.

5.) Heat a large cast-iron skillet or griddle on high.

6.) Generously season patties on both sides with salt and pepper.

7.) Cook burgers for one to two minutes.

8.) Flip and top each with cheese; cover and cook one to two minutes more.

9.) Place burgers on buns and serve with desired toppings.

Coconut Bread Pudding

Serves 6

Ingredients

2 tablespoons (30 g) of butter

1/3 cup (35 g) confectioner's (powdered) sugar

1 cup (200 g) white sugar

4 eggs

1 egg yolk

(2) 14-oz (350 g) cans of coconut cream

1 teaspoon cinnamon

¼ teaspoon ground nutmeg

¼ teaspoon salt

2 tablespoons coconut extract

1 teaspoon (5 mL) almond extract

1 ½ (200 g) cups unsweetened, flaked coconut

½ (50 g) cup fresh coconut

1 pound (450 g) day-old white or French bread cut into 1-inch (2.5 cm) cubes

Directions

1.) Preheat oven to 325°F (165°C). Grease a 9x13-inch (23x32 cm) baking dish with butter, and dust with confectioners' sugar.

2.) In a large bowl, combine sugar, eggs, egg yolk, coconut milk, cinnamon, nutmeg, salt and extracts. Mix until smooth.

3.) Stir in 1 cup (150 g) of flaked coconut, and 1/2 cup (50 g) fresh coconut.

4.) Fold in bread cubes until evenly coated.

5.) Pour into prepared baking dish. Let it macerate for thirty minutes.

6.) Bake on a cookie sheet in preheated oven for twenty-five minutes.

7.) Sprinkle top with remaining 1/2 cup flaked coconut.

8.) Continue baking for twenty-five to thirty minutes, or until center springs back when lightly tapped.

Fettuccine with Scallops
Serves 4

Ingredients

1/4 bag of dry fettuccine or linguine pasta

3 defrosted or fresh large scallops

2 tablespoons (30 mL) olive oil

3 gloves garlic minced

1/4 cup (40 g) diced red bell pepper

3/4 cup (110 g) cherry or small yellow tomatoes

2 tablespoons chopped basil

1 tablespoon chopped thyme and parsley (optional)

Salt and pepper to taste

Directions

1.) Wash scallops under cold water and pat dry with paper towel. Season with salt and pepper.

2.) Heat pan to medium-high.

3.) Put one tablespoon olive oil into pan and add scallops. Cook until brown (about two-three minutes). Flip and cook an additional two minutes.

4.) Remove scallops from pan and let them rest.

5.) Boil pasta in unsalted water until al dente (about seven minutes).

6.) In the pan used for cooking the scallops, add remaining olive oil, garlic, red peppers, tomatoes, salt and pepper. Sauté for approximately five minutes on medium heat. Or until peppers have begun to soften.

7.) Add basil, thyme and parsley and cook for an additional two minutes. Add scallops to the pan to warm them up. After draining the pasta, combine it with scallops and vegetables. Garnish with fresh herbs.

Creamy Coleslaw
Serves 8

Ingredients

2 cups (475 mL) mayonaise

1 cup (240 mL) buttermilk

3 tablespoons (45 mL) white sugar

1 tablespoon celery seeds

1 teaspoon (5 mL) apple cider vinegar

(2) 16-oz (300 g) packages of shredded cabbage/coleslaw mix

Directions

1.) In a large bowl, stir together the mayonnaise, buttermilk, sugar, celery seeds, and vinegar.

2.) Fold in the coleslaw mix.

3.) Refrigerate for a few hours before serving.

Jicama and Cucumber Salad

Serves 4

Ingredients

1 medium jicama, quartered and sliced about
1/4-inch (6 mm) thick

1 cucumber, quartered and sliced about
1/4 inch (6 mm) thick

1 8oz. can of mandarin oranges, drained

juice of two limes

1/2 teaspoon (2.5 mL) ground chili powder

1/2 teaspoon sweet paprika

Directions

1.) In a large bowl, toss jicama, cucumber, lime juice,
and spices together until vegetables are coated.

2.) Sprinkle with sea salt before serving.

SELECTED RESOURCES BY
BOBBY FLAY
★

Books

Bobby Flay's Barbecue Addiction. New York: Clarkson Potter, 2013.

Bobby Flay's Burgers, Fries, and Shakes. New York: Random House, 2014.

Bobby Flay's Grill It! New York: Clarkson Potter, 2008.

Bobby Flay's Mesa Grill Cookbook: Explosive Flavors from the Southwestern Kitchen. New York: Clarkson Potter, 2007.

Bobby Flay's Throwdown! More Than 100 Recipes from Food Network's Ultimate Cooking Challenge. New York: Clarkson Potter, 2008.

Websites

bobbyflay.com

Restaurants

Bar Americain

Bobby Flay Steak

Bobby's Burger Palace

Gato

Mesa Grill

CHRONOLOGY

⭐

December 10, 1964 — Bobby Flay born in New York City.

1982 — Works at Joe Allen's.

1983-84 — Attends French Culinary Institute in New York City.

1986 — Works for Jonathan Waxman; is introduced to Southwestern cuisine.

1988 — Works as executive chef at Miracle Grill.

1991 — Opens Mesa Grill.

1991 — Marries Deborah Ponzek.

1993 — Opens Bolo Grill.

1993 — Divorces Deborah Ponzek.

1993 — French Culinary Institute Outstanding Graduate Award.

1993 — Wins James Beard Foundation's Rising Chef of the Year Award.

1995 — Marries Kate Connelly.

1996 — *Grillin' and Chillin'* debuts.

1996 — Daughter Sophie is born.

1998 — Divorces Kate Connelly.

2000 — First appearance on *Iron Chef*.

2004 — Mesa Grill Las Vegas opens.

2005 — Bar Americain opens.

2005 — Marries Stephanie March.

2005 — *Iron Chef* America debuts.

2006 — *Throwdown with Bobby Flay* debuts.

2007 — Mesa Grill in Bahamas opens.

2008 — First Bobby's Burger Palace opens.

2008 — Bolo closes.

2009 — Bar Americain Mohegan Sun opens.

2013 — Mesa Grill in New York City closes.

2013 — *Beat Bobby Flay* debuts.

2014 — Gato opens.

2015 — Divorces third wife Stephanie March.

CHAPTER NOTES

Chapter 1:   A Chef Takes Shape

1. "Bobby Flay," Chef's Story, *Heritage Radio Network.org*, October 30, 2013, http://www.heritageradionetwork.com/episodes/4972-Chef-s-Story-Episode-60-Bobby-Flay.
2. Kane, Michael. "All in a Flay's Work." The *New York Post*. May 30, 2011. http://nypost.com/2011/05/30/all-in-a-flays-work/.
3. Berman, Fran. "Interview With Bobby Flay." *StarChefs.com*. 1998. http://www.starchefs.com/BFlay/interview.html.

Chapter 2:   Putting on the Apron

1. "Bobby Flay," Chef's Story, *Heritage Radio Network.org*, October 30, 2013, http://www.heritageradionetwork.com/episodes/4972-Chef-s-Story-Episode-60-Bobby-Flay.
2. Debaise, Colleen. "How a Famous Foodie Got His Start." The *Wall Street Journal*. April 21, 2011. http://www.wsj.com/articles/SB100 01424052748704570704576274822558736018
3. Aagaard, Stephanie Sayfie. "Bobby Flay Talks Food." *OceanDrive*. February 1, 2010. http://oceandrive.com/celebrities/articles/bobby-flay
4. Weigl, Andres. "An interview with celebrity chef Bobby Flay." *Catholic Online*. October 28, 2008. http://www.catholic.org/news/hf/home/story.php?id=30269
5. Lagorio-Chafkin, Christine. "How Bobby Flay Build a Sizzling Empire." *Inc.* April 2015. http://www.inc.com/magazine/201504/christine-lagorio/bobby-flay-how-i-did-it-cooking-with-gas.html
6. Kane, Michael. "All in a Flay's Work." The *New York Post*. May 30, 2011. http://nypost.com/2011/05/30/all-in-a-flays-work/.
7. Krigbaum, Megan. "Interview With TV Chef Bobby Flay." *Food & Wine*. http://www.foodandwine.com/articles/tv-chef-interview-bobby-flay

Chapter 3   The Beginning of an Empire

1. "Grilling Recipes from Bobby Flay." Viking. http://www.vikingrange.com/consumer/lifestyle/article.jsp?id=prod5910172
2. Miller, Bryan. "Restaurants." The *New York Times*. March 29, 1991. http://www.nytimes.com/1991/03/29/arts/restaurants-659191.html
3. Reichl, Ruth. "Restaurants." The *New York Times*. January 7, 1994. http://www.nytimes.com/1994/01/07/arts/restaurants-801020.html
4. Bobby Flay Biography. *Biography.com*. http://www.biography.com/people/bobby-flay-578278
5. "Celebrity Chefs at Home: Bobby Flay." *Delish.com*. January 15, 2009. http://www.biography.com/people/bobby-flay-578278
6. Ibid.
7. Lagorio-Chafkin, Christine. "How Bobby Flay Build a Sizzling Empire." *Inc.* April 2015. http://www.inc.com/magazine/201504/christine-lagorio/bobby-flay-how-i-did-it-cooking-with-gas.html

Chapter 4:   Food Becomes a TV Star

1. Salkin, Allen. *From Scratch: Inside the Food Network.* (New York: G.P. Putnam's Sons, 2013)
2. Ponzek, Debra. *The Dinnertime Survival Cookbook.* (Philadelphia, PA: Running Press, 2013.)
3. Brady, Lois Smith. "Vows." The *New York Times*. October 15, 1995. http://www.nytimes.com/1995/10/15/style/vows-kate-connelly-and-bobby-flay.html
4. Ibid.
5. Lagorio-Chafkin, Christine. "How Bobby Flay Build a Sizzling Empire." *Inc.* April 2015. http://www.inc.com/magazine/201504/christine-lagorio/bobby-flay-how-i-did-it-cooking-with-gas.html

6. Krigbaum, Megan. "Interview With TV Chef Bobby Flay." *Food & Wine*. http://www.foodandwine.com/articles/tv-chef-interview-bobby-flay

7. Bogdanovich, Peter. "Craig Kilborn's Replacement? ... Grilling Bobby Flay ... Naomi Unzipped; Malcolm-Jamal on Magic" *New York Observer*. July 20, 1998. http://observer.com/1998/07/craig-kilborns-replacement-grilling-bobby-flay-naomi-unzipped-malcolmjamal-on-magic/

Chapter 5: Entering the Arena of Iron Chef

1. Grimes, William. "Samurai of Cuisine, on a New Battlefield." The *New York Times*. January 14, 2005. http://www.nytimes.com/2005/01/14/arts/television/samurai-of-cuisine-on-a-new-battlefield.html

2. Krigbaum, Megan. "Interview With TV Chef Bobby Flay." *Food & Wine*. http://www.foodandwine.com/articles/tv-chef-interview-bobby-flay

Chapter 6: Keeping the TV Screen Cooking

1. Spencer, Kathleen. "Giada de Laurentiis and Bobby Flay Talk About Family and Food with Rachael Ray." *Momtastic*. http://www.momtastic.com/life/172675-giada-de-laurentiis-and-bobby-flay-talk-family-and-food-with-rachael-ray/

2. "What Does it Take To Beat Bobby Flay? Special Guests Speak Out." *Food Network*. http://www.foodnetwork.com/shows/beat-bobby-flay/what-does-it-take-to-beat-bobby-flay-special-guests-speak-out.html

Chapter 7: Cooking and Beyond

1. Sifton, Sam. "Review: Bar Americain." The *New York Times*. May 25, 2010. http://events.nytimes.com/2010/05/26/dining/reviews/26dinbriefs.html

2. Bovino, Arthur. "The B-Team: Chef Bobby Flay Talks About the Secret to His Success." The *Daily Meal*. February 21, 2015. http://

www.thedailymeal.com/eat/b-team-chef-bobby-flay-talks-about-secret-his-success

3. Galarraga, Joe. "30 x 30: Bobby Flay." *Radio Heritage Network.* http://www.heritageradionetwork.org/category_posts/392-30x30-Bobby-Flay

4. Ibid.

5. Wells, Pete. "A Glimpse (And a Taste) of Celebrity." The *New York Times.* June 10, 2014.

6. Richman, Alan. "A Celebrity Chef Gets it Right" *GQ.* April 29, 2014. http://www.gq.com/life/food/201405/alan-richman-gato

7. Cuozzo, Steve. "New NOHO Mediterranean Restaurant is Bobby Flay's Best." *New York Post.* April 24, 2014. http://nypost.com/2014/04/24/new-noho-mediterranean-restaurant-is-bobby-flays-best/

8. Russo, Maria. "What's it Like to Be Friends with Bobby Flay, According to Michael Symon." *foodnetwork.com.* July 6, 2014. http://blog.foodnetwork.com/fn-dish/2014/07/what-its-like-to-be-friends-with-bobby-flay-according-to-michael-symon/

9. "Bobby Flay," Chef's Story, *Heritage Radio Network.org*, October 30, 2013, http://www.heritageradionetwork.com/episodes/4972-Chef-s-Story-Episode-60-Bobby-Flay.

10. Galarraga, Joe. "30 x 30: Bobby Flay." *Radio Heritage Network.* http://www.heritageradionetwork.org/category_posts/392-30x30-Bobby-Flay

chiffonade—A cutting method for herbs or green leafy vegetables to create thin strips of ribbons

crostata—An Italian baked tart or pie

executive chef—Also called chef manager, this is the person in charge of the kitchen in a restaurant

expediter—The person in charge of setting the pace and flow in the kitchen. He or she makes sure that orders are completed together and on time.

flambé—Prepared in flaming liquor, especially brandy.

julienne—A cutting technique to create small, matchlike pieces.

line chef—Also called a station chef or chef de partie, this person works under the executive chef or sous chef. These chefs are responsible for prepping ingredients and putting together dishes according to restaurant recipes and specifications. Line chefs usually work on specific station, such as the grill, stove, or vegetable prep area.

marinade—A sauce in which meat, fish, or vegetables are soaked to enrich the food with flavor before cooking.

paella—A Spanish dish of rice and many other ingredients, usually seafood and sometimes chicken or sausage. Typically, flavored with saffron and cooked in a large shallow pan.

rub—A spice and/or herb mixture that is added to foods (typically meats) before cooking.

sautée—To fry or brown quickly in a very hot pan with a small amount of fat, butter, or oil.

sous chef—The chef who is second-in-command of the kitchen, below the executive or head chef.

tamale—A Mexican food that features seasoned meat, seafood, or vegetables packed in a cornmeal dough and steamed in a corn husk.

tournée—A method of cutting and peeling root vegetables so they have a small football-shaped appearance.

vinaigrette—A salad dressing made from oil, vinegar, and seasonings.

FURTHER READING

Books

The Cookbook for Teens. Mendocino, CA: Mendocino Press, 2014

Locricchio, Matthew. *Teen Cuisine*. Seattle, WA: Skyscape, 2014.

Marchive, Laurane. *The Green Teen Cookbook*. San Francisco, CA: Zest Books, 2014.

Salkin, Allen. *From Scratch: Inside the Food Network*. New York, NY: G.P. Putnam's Sons, 2013.

Websites

Cooking Teens

cookingteens.com

Healty and tasty recipes for young chefs, as well as articles on young people involved with cooking.

Teen Recipes

teen-recipes.com

A wealth of delicious and simple recipes that teens can prepare.

Movies

Chef. Directed by Jon Favreau. 2014.

The Hundred-Foot Journey. Directed by Lasse Hallström. 2014.

INDEX